MW00633560

ENDORSEMENT

When our negative belief systems are not resisted but rather cultivated in the dwelling place of our hearts and mind, the soil of our decision-making becomes rooted in lies and produces destructive fruit in our lives. The truth is this: when repentance consists of Believers rushing to the altar to repent for their beliefs, and not just what they have done wrong, that is the day we will see real transformation. Steve Backlund's new book Fully Convinced: The Art of Decision Making will equip you to conquer the doubt-devil and help you become a confident decision-maker. If you are ready to break off lies and see the dreams of your life fulfilled, this book is for you!

Kris Vallotton
Senior Associate Leader, Bethel Church, Redding, CA
Co-Founder of Bethel School of Supernatural Ministry
Author of fifteen books, including *The Supernatural Ways of Royalty and Uprising.*

STEVE BACKLUND

FULLY CONVINCED

THE ART OF
DECISION MAKING

Fully Convinced: The Art of Decision Making
Copyright 2022 by Steve Backlund, Igniting Hope Ministries
www.ignitinghope.com

ISBN - 978-1-7363601-5-6

All rights reserved. This book is protected by the copyright laws of the United States of America. This book may not be copied or reprinted for commercial gain or profit. The use of short quotations or occasional page copying for personal or group study is permitted and encouraged. Unless otherwise identified, Scripture quotations are from the New King James Version. Copyright 1982 by Thomas Nelson, Inc. Used by permission. All rights reserved. All emphasis within Scripture (besides italics) is the author's own. Please note that the author's publishing style capitalizes certain pronouns in Scripture that refer to the Father, Son, and Holy Spirit, and may differ from other publisher's styles."

Cover image credit: Makhbubakhon Ismatova
Cover design: Annalisa Gilbert & Zoltan Hercik
Interior layout and formatting: Eugene Rijn Saratorio

Many thanks to following who helped with editing this book: Shelter Musavengana, Will Winter, Ash Anderson, Jessica-Jean Winter, Becky Cancelosi, Claire Huestis, Vicki Macfarlane, and to the first Fully Convinced course students who caught errors and provided feedback to us on the book's content.

If you enjoy this book and want more, go to ignitinghope.com to find:

- Blogs and podcasts
- Books and resources
- Information on the Backlunds' speaking itinerary
- The contact form for Steve or Wendy about speaking to your group
- Many free resources to inspire your life
- Online events to ignite your hope

CONTENTS

INTRODUCTION

"For whom He foreknew, He also predestined to be conformed to the image of His Son" (Romans 8:29).

For believers, God's grace is working powerfully to conform us into Christ-likeness. For most of my faith journey, I thought this becoming more like Jesus was only in my behavior and in having "Christian" attitudes. I now know it also includes how we think. As God matures us, we will become increasingly and fully convinced about God's promises, our identity in Christ, and that what we are doing is right and significant.

Fully Convinced: The Art of Decision-Making is a life-changing book. I believe it is the most important book I have written yet. Its content combines my teachings on hope, victorious mindsets, joy, declarations, and empowerment with fresh insights on how to make decisions and how to attach faith to what we decide to do.

I bless you as you read this book. My prayer for you is that you will be more confident than ever before in your decisions and beliefs.

Unreasonably optimistic,
Steve Backlund

ABOUT THE AUTHOR

Steve Backlund is an encourager, leader developer, joy activist, and a revivalist teacher. He has a unique gift to release hope and joy in his speaking, writings, and in his leadership. Steve and his wife Wendy were senior pastors for seventeen years and now reside in Redding, CA. He is the Associate Director of the Bethel Leaders Network, and with his wife Wendy founded Igniting Hope Ministries and the Igniting Hope Academy. The Backlunds have three children and seven grand-children.

"Steve Backlund is known for his wisdom and practical insights on how to do life." The students in our ministry school, Bethel School of Supernatural Ministry, love him because he always leaves them encouraged and refreshed in their vision. He has an unusual gift to take the mundane and make it exciting and to take the familiar and make it new."

Bill Johnson, Bethel Church, Redding,
CA - Author of <u>When Heaven Invades Earth</u>

CHAPTER 1

The Epidemic of Doubt, Insecurity, and Guilt

How do we change the trajectory of our lives? How do we really experience Romans 12:2 of being transformed by the renewing of our minds? How can the truth actually make us free?

One of the ways we can do this is to ask ourselves specific questions which have the potential to bring life-changing revelation. For me, the following questions have caused me to see what my biggest problem is (my beliefs).

1. Is my feeling of unworthiness a bigger problem than what I feel unworthy about?
2. Is my feeling of shame a bigger problem than what I feel ashamed about?
3. Is my feeling of regret a bigger problem than what I feel regret about?
4. Is my unresolved doubt about a decision or commitment I have made a bigger problem than the decision or commitment itself?
5. Is my belief that God is more interested in my obedience over enjoying my relationship with Him a bigger problem than what I am doing wrong in my life?

6. When I take communion, is my tendency to focus on what is wrong with me a bigger problem than what is wrong with me?

I believe the answer to these questions is almost always yes. This chapter and this book will help make my case for this belief. Even if you decide not to agree with all of my conclusions, I still will hopefully have accomplished one of my main goals for you as the reader, which is to inspire you to think through what you really believe about how God wants us to think and feel about who we are and what we do.

If we don't know what our problem is, then we have a real problem! This is a book that will help us recognize, in a deeper way, the importance of prioritizing our beliefs as the key to breakthrough and seeing our dreams fulfilled. It will help many overcome what I call the epidemic of negative emotions that result from believing lies.

What is an epidemic? It is an outbreak of disease that spreads quickly and affects many individuals at the same time. Even though it is more commonly associated with physical illnesses, I have witnessed another kind of longstanding epidemic among the body of Christ. I am not talking about an epidemic of compromise or sinful behaviors, but of doubt, insecurity, guilt, shame, and unworthiness. This "dis-ease" causes many to lack confidence in who they are, what they are doing, what they can do, and in being fully convinced they are in right standing with God and are celebrated and greatly loved by Him.

There are so many believers who feel they are not committed enough to God, who feel they are not doing enough, or who feel less than others, doubt themselves, negatively compare themselves to others, feel guilty for not giving enough, not praying enough, or not being sincere enough.

Someone might say, "But what if it is true that we really are not sincere or committed to God enough? Won't this teaching just give people an excuse to continue in those ways?" This is a great question. Let's talk about that.

The theological beliefs that can create the greatest transformation also have the potential to be used to justify hurtful beliefs and behaviors. Remember, the same culture that created eleven world-changers also produced a Judas who betrayed Jesus. If our goal in leadership is to prevent a Judas, we will most likely not produce world changers. In the same way, If we are fixated on preventing bad behavior by mainly focusing on what is wrong with us, we will block greatness from manifesting in and through us.

Certainly, we need healthy relational accountability to ensure we are not abusing others or heading in destructive personal directions. Yes, we may need counseling or inner healing, but this needs to be a part of a plan to overcome the lies creating doubt, shame, inferiority, and an overall lack of confidence; not a replacement for it.

I used to think my doubt, insecurity, and feelings of insignificance were my personality and my predestined lot in life. I believed I was at a disadvantage in life compared to more "successful" people. What I have discovered is that these feelings were the result of believing lies. And what I did not understand was that these feelings were "common to man" (1 Corinthians 10:13). Everyone is tempted to believe lies that lead to feeling depressed.

The greatest temptations we face are not to do wrong but to believe wrong. "No temptation has overtaken you except such as is common to man; but God is faithful, who will not allow you to be tempted beyond what you are able . . ." (1 Corinthians 10:13). Eve's first temptation in the garden was to believe the lie that God was not good. She embraced this deception and then sinned in her actions. Jesus' temptations in the wilderness in Matthew 4 were enticing Him to doubt His true identity ("If you are the Son of God . . .").

The real spiritual warfare is whether we are going to believe lies or truth. "The truth will make you free" (John 8:32). Truth makes us free first in our emotions and then in our circumstances. Lies restrict us first in our emotions and then in our circumstances. This epidemic of doubt, insecurity, and guilt comes from believing lies. And the good news is that we are empowered by God to decide to believe what is true. Unfortunately, many, like my dog, Buddy, live indecisively and miss the power of being fully convinced in what to believe and do.

Buddy, Will You Just Decide!

My dog, Buddy, often struggles with whether he wants to be in the house or out of the house. He frequently will be outside our kitchen door barking to come into the house. When we open the door, Buddy will often stay outside undecided about if he really wants to come in. Whenever this happens, I am thinking, "Buddy, will you just decide!"

Elijah had a similar thought for a much more important situation concerning the Children of Israel. "How long halt ye between two opinions? If the Lord be God, follow Him; but if Baal, then follow him" (1 Kings 18:21 KJV).

I am fascinated by the way, "How long halt ye between two opinions", is translated in other Bible versions:

- "How long will you hesitate between two opinions?" (AMP)
- "How long will you waver between two opinions?" (CSB)
- "How much longer will you try to have things both ways?" (CEV)

- "How long will you keep jumping from one side to the other?" (ERV)
- "How long will you be stuck between two points of view?" (NCB)
- "How long will you not decide between two choices?" (NCV)

Elijah the Prophet challenged the people to decide and become fully convinced, one way or the other, concerning who they were to follow (Baal or God). He asked them, "How long are you going to be indecisive and waver between the two options you have? Make a decision!"

Certainly, the most important decision we will ever make is whether or not we believe in and receive Jesus as our Lord and Savior, but Elijah's question has spoken to me in many other areas where I have been indecisive, doubting, and/or wavering between options. Some of these areas are:

- **Financial Decisions** - I waver regarding whether I should spend (or have spent) a certain amount of money.

- **Identity** - I waver between believing who God says I am and believing who my feelings and past experience say I am.

- **Commitments, Relationships, and Responsibilities** - I have struggled at different times in my life doubting whether I should be in the job I am in, invest in certain relationships, or have committed to doing certain things.

- **God's Feelings Toward Me** - I have wavered between believing whether God loves me or not.

One day the Lord asked me the same question Elijah asked the Israelites, "Steve, how long are you going to live in doubt and double-mindedness about these things? Will you just decide!"

My answer was, "Lord, I am trying, but it does not seem easy to do."

Sincere Christians often struggle the most with doubt and double-mindedness. This indecisiveness comes from a fear of making the wrong choice or fear of change. When we embrace these fears, it becomes easier to avoid making decisions. What we need to understand is that not deciding is a decision. We are choosing not to choose. It's one of the methods our subconscious uses to maintain our status quo. Just like Buddy, our doubt neutralizes forward movement.

Doubt is a crippler of our confidence and effectiveness. It is the opposite of being fully convinced. We all battle with some level of doubt. James 1:6-8 talks about it, "But let him ask (for wisdom) in faith, with no doubting, for he who doubts is like a wave of the sea driven and tossed by the wind . . . for he is a double-minded man unstable in all his ways."

So how can we overcome the "Buddy syndrome" and confidently decide what we are going to do and believe? Here are some ideas that will help:

1. Become convinced it is crucial to overcome doubt and double-mindedness.
2. Believe and declare we can do it. God never asks us to do anything He has not empowered us to do.
3. Thank God regularly that we are receiving a constant flow of wisdom and revelation (and that we will always know what to do).
4. Get a good process of decision-making and then decide (attach faith to) what you are going to do and believe. This book will help you greatly in doing this.

"Buddy, will you just decide!"

But here is the bigger question God asked me. "Steve, how long will you waver in what you believe about Me, yourself, others, and concerning what you are doing? When will you stop wavering between different choices and move toward truly deciding?"

My Struggles

My most powerful teachings have come from my own struggles. Scripture teaches us that we have authority in whatever area we are overcoming or have overcome. "Blessed is the man who endures temptation; for when he has been approved, he will receive the crown of life which the Lord has promised to those who love Him" (James 1:12). I believe a crown of life is authority for us to give life to others in the area we have overcome. Our struggles in life are not just about us, but they are an indicator of the areas where our greatest influence will be in the future. This certainly has been true for me in decision-making. My seeming inability to be decisive has forced me to find God's wisdom and strength, plus it has given me compassion for others who battle the same issue.

Here are three major struggles from my life and the truths I learned from them.

Doubting My Salvation

I became a follower of Jesus at age 19, and I started attending church regularly then. My belief system at that time was that if I came to church and did not feel saved, then I wasn't saved. So I would go up to the altar and get saved again. Then the Lord said, "Steve, I have good news for you. You are saved even when you don't feel saved." I thought, "Wow, that is amazing! I thought feelings were the highest indicator of truth there was." Even after hearing this, I would still come to church not feeling saved. They would give the altar call to be saved, and every time

I very much wanted to respond and go to the front. But, the Lord would say, "Do not go down there. Stay, Steve! Stay in your seat." I would say, "But, Lord, if I go down there, I know I'll break off the spirit of heaviness from my life." One day He said, "I'm going to show you how to break the spirit of heaviness off yourself, and it is not by *doing* something different but by *believing* something different." I was learning that feelings don't validate truth; they just validate what we believe to be true. Just because I don't feel something is true that God says I am, or that He says I can do, doesn't mean it's not true. I am still righteous in Him even if I don't feel righteous. I am still powerful even if I don't feel powerful. Navigating through this situation of doubting my salvation helped me not trust feelings as the indicator of what is true or not.

Marriage Proposal to Wendy

My decision to marry Wendy briefly sent me into a negative emotional decision-making tailspin. It was a season where I had a great fear of making wrong decisions. My sincerity for God worked against me because I felt that God's will for my life was very narrow, and I probably would not be able to fully know or obey it. I focused on Old Testament verses like Jeremiah 17:9, "The heart is deceitful above all things, and desperately wicked; who can know it?" This belief created an inability to attach faith to what I was doing. In our situation, Wendy and I had been dating when we became saved, and soon after, we decided to break up so that we could focus on our relationship with God and build a solid foundation in purity and other areas. We felt that God had asked us to do this. After about a year, we slowly began seeing each other again (having Coke or a coffee together). We felt this was not right because of what we believed God had told us in the past. So we went to our youth pastor to talk to him about it, and he asked us if we had prayed about getting married. What he asked us surprised us, but we said we would do it. The next weekend we prayed and fasted to hear God, and then we met on that Sunday afternoon to discuss what we had each heard. We discovered that both of us had gotten the answer "Yes, we were to get married". It was not the most romantic proposal, but it was special. After that, I drove off in my Volkswagen bus and felt like every demon in the state of California got into the bus with me and they were saying, "What if you're wrong? What if you're wrong?" As I listened to that, I went into emotional chaos. I tried to find some of my mentors to help me but nobody was available. I knew it would have been dumb to say something to Wendy so I decided to go to our church's prayer house to pray. I started rehearsing all the reasons why I had believed the Lord said yes. I was talking to God and myself loudly (sometimes we have to get violent against lies). As I passionately recalled my "God story" for why I had said yes, I broke off the doubt and experienced peace and confidence to get married. I attached faith to my decision to marry Wendy, and forty-plus years later, I am still so glad I did. This situation helped me build the habit of fighting my double-mindedness by rehearsing what I believe I've heard or been told.

Doubting I Should Continue Pastoring

My first senior pastorate was in the desert near Las Vegas, Nevada. It was not logical for many reasons to go there in the first place, but Wendy and I had a strong word (Matthew 4:4) that we were to be there. After a few years, I began to doubt that word because of the challenges I was facing and because I was not being as successful as I thought I was supposed to be. So I told the Lord I needed a fresh word to live from and to help me remain in Nevada in faith. As I was praying I had this thought, "Steve, I haven't called you to fail, I've called you to succeed." I didn't tell anyone this. It was a good word, but it wasn't strong enough to help me overcome the doubts I had. Soon after, I went to a meeting with fellow pastors in my region, and I shared with them that I was battling discouragement and I needed their prayers. They gathered around me and laid hands on me. The first person to pray over me said these words, "Father, I thank you that you haven't called Steve to fail; you called him to succeed." Wow! It was one of the most important moments of my whole life. I thought, "That's God! That's gotta be God!" And it was a word that helped me defeat the lies that I was believing. Matthew 4:4 says "Man shall not live by bread alone but by every word that proceeds from the mouth of God..." The quality of our lives depends on identifying what God has told us. Ephesians 6:17 says, "Take up the sword of the Spirit which is the word of God..." I took up that word that God hadn't called me to fail, and that He had called me to succeed. I spoke it aloud over and over to battle the lies that were creating my doubts, insecurity, and unworthiness. This situation helped me to believe God for a fresh word to fight doubt.

Why the Struggle with Doubt, Insecurity, and Guilt?

The above examples are three of many internal battles I have had that have contributed to a lack of confidence in who I was and what I was doing. As I considered the root issues in me that contributed to my struggles, I recognized two beliefs that were especially problematic for me: 1) I was not doing enough to be confident or blessed, and 2) I deserved to feel shameful about who I was. Let's explore each of these.

The Never Enough Lie

There is a message that the enemy of our souls repeatedly speaks. It has effectively drained life and joy out of multitudes. This message comes in thoughts and words that are designed to drive us to be our own hard taskmasters, with our perceived failures ever before us. Behind it all, the enemy is saying something much more damaging: "You aren't doing enough right things to be worthy of being blessed, approved by the Father, or significant."

We have all heard or thought things like these:

- You are not good enough
- You are not committed to God enough
- You are not giving enough
- You are not sorry enough
- Your family is not good enough
- You don't love God enough
- You don't have enough money or quality people around you to make a difference
- You don't have enough faith
- You don't have enough education or skills
- You haven't prayed, read your Bible, or fasted enough
- You have not obeyed God enough
- You have not forgiven enough
- You have not shared the gospel enough
- You have not given your loved ones enough time
- You have not been consistent enough

Certainly, we are to keep growing and allow ourselves to be challenged to do more, but if we are not careful, we will never be able to attach faith to what we are doing because we are condemning ourselves by believing we are never doing enough.

Which is more effective?

- Praying five minutes a day in faith or praying for an hour but feeling like you should have prayed more?
- Giving your kids 30 quality, faith-filled minutes or giving them two hours but believing you aren't as good of a parent as your neighbor?

Scripture teaches us that whatever we do without faith is sin (Romans 14:23), so the answer to the above questions is obvious. Again, the desire to grow and do more is important, but we cannot grow effectively if we constantly feel bad about ourselves and our progress. Besides, how much is really enough? Who gets to decide that? Well, I am glad you asked. Surprisingly, we get to decide what is enough. Here are two passages to consider that support this:

1. "But each one must give as he has decided in his heart" (2 Corinthians 9:7).
2. "Do you have faith? Have it to yourself before God. **Happy is he who does not condemn himself** in what he approves. But he who doubts is condemned if he eats, because he does not eat from faith; for whatever is not from faith is sin" (Romans 14:22-23).

It is this second passage I want to focus on here. "Happy is he who does not condemn himself in what he approves" (Romans 14:23). It is not God condemning us that makes us unhappy, but it is our condemning ourselves that is the problem. When we declare war on this self-condemnation, we will find a key to overcoming the "never enough lie," and a whole host of other life-draining falsehoods.

Romans 14 is a life-launching chapter for those who desire emotional health and increased positive influence. One of the chapter's main points is to attach faith to what you do. The chapter ends with the gold-mine verses 22 and 23 where we glean:

- Happy is he who does not condemn himself.
- Doubt in our choices (which includes feeling like we are not doing enough) leads to our condemning ourselves.
- Whatever we do without attaching faith misses the mark (is sin) - the "you are not doing enough" lie is one of the main reasons we are tempted to live in doubt about what we are doing.

We cannot end without saying this: **Jesus has done enough!** Every time we participate in communion, we remember what He has done. "Looking unto Jesus, the author and finisher of our faith" (Hebrews 12:2). As we continue to receive the revelation of His victory over death, sin, and demonic principalities, and as we gain more knowledge of our born-again identity in Him, we will find the most important response to the "you are not doing enough" lie: "Jesus has done enough because I could not." Now that is good news.

God's grace is empowering you now to defeat the "never enough" lie by attaching faith to what you are doing and by standing firmly on the finished work of Jesus. We rejoice together in this. Now let's demolish another stronghold: shame.

Defeating Unsuspected Sources of Shame

Shame is a painful feeling of humiliation or distress caused by the consciousness of wrong or foolish behavior. It is a wound in our soul that, if not healed, will cause us to feel unworthy to be blessed or significant.

When I think of shame, my mind usually goes to big mistakes or sins one has committed (or those committed against them) that cause great regret, embarrassment, and feelings of being less than others. Even though this deep shame is something we need to help people with, I want to address some unsuspected sources of shame that practically everyone faces.

I have recently taken an inventory of areas of my life where I have experienced shame. The shame I felt concerning these was not a major humiliation or distress, but it manifested in embarrassment, feeling inferior to others, and in concluding I was not worthy to be radically blessed or greatly happy. It is this kind of shame I want to discuss here and its sources. I have listed some below that most of us will be able to relate to.

Common sources of shame that cause us to feel less than, embarrassed, and unworthy:

1. **Appearance Shame** – Almost everyone has things about their appearance they do not like. As we compare ourselves to airbrushed models, we all come up short. Advertisements and the media are unrelenting in their depiction of what beauty is and none of us reach it.

2. **Family Situation Shame** – This is another area where few do not have potential shame-inducing situations. Whether it is singleness, divorce, addictions, being childless, abuse, adult children not following Jesus, or other dysfunctions, family dynamics can be shame-producers.

3. **Life Accomplishments Shame** – As people get older, many battle shame for not having done more with their lives.

4. **Education Shame** – Numerous people feel bad for not going further in school and feel less than those with higher education.

5. **Vocation Shame** – Society esteems some vocations highly while it also labels others as lesser jobs to have. If we are employed in a non-esteemed job for our age, we will most likely fight some level of shame for that.

6. **Spiritual Gifts Shame** – The church tends to exalt those with public ministry gifts or who have a great anointing to see dramatic things happen. Those called into such things as administration and pastoring, and those that function in the

gift of helps (1 Corinthians 12:28) can feel inferior for not doing "spectacular" things.

7. **Embarrassing Things We Have Done Shame** – We have all done stupid things. Whether it is tripping in front of a group of people, saying something dumb, or something else, we can be tempted to negatively rehearse embarrassing moments over and over.

8. **Possessions Shame** – Examples of this are our cars, our houses, the clothes we wear, jewelry, furniture, phones or gadgets, types of vacations we take, etc.

9. **Christian Commitment and Good Works Shame** – Many walk in shame because they do not believe they are committed to God enough or they think they are not doing enough good works. Shame, condemnation, and guilt are not God's instruments to draw people or bring someone closer to Him.

What can we do about these unsuspecting sources of shame?

1. **Cultivate Thankfulness for What You Have** – A majority of the people in the world would like to trade places with you.

2. **Recognize Everyone Has to Overcome Some Level of Shame** – There is nothing uniquely wrong with you.

3. **Know Jesus Took Your Shame on the Cross** – He hung naked on a cross taking not only your sins but your shame.

4. **See Shame-Inducing Moments as a Growth Opportunity** – Recognize the moments when you feel inferior, embarrassed,

and unworthy, and see them as opportunities to grow in celebrating who you are, and praying for those who seem to be better than you.

5. **Understand Everyone Has Issues and you Have Something to Offer Every Person** – "The greatest will be the servant of all" (Matthew 23:11).

The "never enough" lie certainly contributes to the unsuspecting sources of shame we feel. As we value and pursue a fully convinced mindset in who we are and what we do, then we will have the opportunity to obliterate the lies fueling this shame, plus regret, insecurity, unworthiness, and feeling powerless.

Conclusion

At the beginning of the chapter, I asked some questions to help us see that our emotional response to what is happening or has happened (shame, indecision, regret, doubt, guilt, etc.) is almost always a bigger problem than what those feelings are resulting from. This revelation is the beginning point on the journey to live a fully convinced, victorious lifestyle. Our next chapter, "The Power of Beliefs", will take this revelation even higher.

CHAPTER 2

The Power of Beliefs

Transformation does not come from surrendering your heart but from surrendering your beliefs.

"Lord, I believe; help my unbelief!"

A father pleaded with Jesus to help his demon-possessed son. "'If You can do anything, have compassion on us and help us.' Jesus said to him, 'If you can believe, all things are possible to him who believes.' Immediately the father of the child cried out and said with tears, 'Lord, I believe; help my unbelief!'" (Mark 9:22-24).

This father received the revelation that his beliefs were the critical factor in what he and his family would experience. In response to this revelation, he asked Jesus for supernatural help to strengthen his faith (beliefs). We would be wise to do the same.

What we believe is the deciding factor in what we will experience. What we believe is ultimately more important than what we do. Romans 12:2 does not say:

- Be transformed by trying harder.
- Be transformed by focusing primarily on your behavior.
- Be transformed by doing something different.

No, it says, "Be transformed by the renewing of your mind." This is believing something higher (what God says) than our feelings and experiences. Transformation is experiencing the promises of God (of Christ-likeness in behavior, power, security, and influence).

What Jesus basically said to the pleading father was, "You are not a victim of a reluctant or hindered God. You are a powerful person who can change circumstances and make a tremendous impact through what you believe." The father understood this and asked Jesus to help him grow in his faith.

Our faith is meant to get stronger and stronger. It is designed for growth and increase. This growth is part of being sanctified and conformed into the image of Christ (Hebrews 10:14, Romans 8:29).

Abraham is our example to follow in progressively getting stronger in believing. "(Abraham) did not waver at the promise of God through unbelief **but was strengthened in faith,** giving glory to God, and being **fully convinced** that what He had promised He was also able to perform" (Romans 4:20-21).

"Abraham did not waver . . ." From my perspective, it looks like Abraham had some big waverings, but God looks at our faith journey differently than we do. Just because we are not yet fully convinced in an area of life does not necessarily mean we are doing something wrong. This is an important concept to understand as we pursue being fully convinced. We do not wait for perfection to celebrate our beliefs, we celebrate our growth.

How do we ensure our faith is being strengthened? Let's look at two important verses. "Be transformed by the renewing of your mind" (Romans 12:2), and "Looking unto Jesus, the author and finisher of our faith" (Hebrews 12:2). It is important to understand that in our "renewing the mind" journey, our faith is to be more focused on God's completing power ("finisher of our faith") than in our ability to believe right. We truly fix our eyes on Jesus, eagerly expecting to see His goodness in our lives.

What then are the areas of our lives that we can expect to be strengthened and led into being fully convinced? Here are five:

- **Theological Conclusions** – "One person esteems *one* day above another; another esteems every day alike. Let each be **fully convinced** in his own mind" (Romans 14:5). We are being strengthened toward being fully convinced in our doctrinal beliefs. The Bible is clear on the most important matters about what is right or wrong, but in some areas of life, there can be a difference in the interpretation of God's will. In some situations like what is mentioned in Romans 14:5, two people can have a different conclusion and both be right.

- **God's Promises to Us** – "He did not waver at the promise of God through unbelief, but was strengthened in faith, giving glory to God, and being **fully convinced** that what He had promised He was also able to perform" (Romans 4:20-21). We have already mentioned this verse, but I could not resist having you read it again.

- **Our Assignments and Decisions** – "Then the Spirit told me to go with them, **doubting nothing**" (Acts 11:12). Like Peter, we will do seemingly illogical things because we have a big God story that causes us to be convinced we are going in the right direction.

- **The Amount We Give of Ourselves to Something** – "So let each one give as he purposes in his heart, not grudgingly or of necessity; for God loves a cheerful giver" (2 Corinthians 9:7). We are being strengthened to consistently decide cheerfully what to give or not to give in money, commitments, time, etc.

- **Answered Prayer About Wisdom** – "But let him ask in faith, **with no doubting**, for he who doubts is like a wave of the sea driven and tossed by the wind" (James 1:6). Jesus is perfecting our faith to believe we will always know what to do in every situation.

Look through this list again. You can expect to become fully convinced about each of these five aspects of your life. This is exciting. "Father, thank You that you are finishing our faith and beliefs about these areas in an incredible way."

Besides the five areas listed above, we will be strengthened in our identity beliefs (who we believe we are) and in what we will be doing in the future. Here is a normal progression concerning our identity, God's callings and the assignments He has for us. It is illustrated in the lives of Abraham and Sarah (Genesis 12-21) and in the life of Gideon (Judges 6 - 8).

1. **It's Ridiculous** – if we are not hearing a word from the Lord that is very contrary to our past experience, we are not hearing high enough promises for ourselves.

2. **It's Possible** – we know we are starting to believe when our hope level starts to rise.

3. **It's Probable** – we do not give up, and our faith is being strengthened.

4. **I'm Fully Convinced** – even though the promise has not happened yet, I know it will.

"Lord, I believe; help my unbelief." "Thank you, Lord, for helping us be fully convinced people." As we allow Him to strengthen our beliefs, we will not only see breakthrough in our own lives, but we will become the answer to the needs of the world around us.

Surrendering Our Beliefs

Wendy and I basically lived in Romans 12:1 for the first fifteen years of our Christian life. It is such a great verse. It says to "sacrifice our bodies as a living sacrifice" to the Lord. It is so important to do that. This means surrendering our hearts and wills to God and making Him not only our Savior, but our Lord, "Not my will be done but Your will be done" (Luke 22:42). For us, it was a season of learning to do things God's way. I have never submitted an area of my life to God and then said, "I wish I had not done it God's way." His ways are perfect and will bless our lives.

After those powerful fifteen years, in 1991 we moved to the desert near Las Vegas, Nevada to pastor a church. God seems to like to send people to deserts to teach them how to repent, and the best definition of repentance is to change the way you think. It was there that we heard this, "Steve and Wendy, I love your heart for Romans 12:1, but if you are going to see transformation, I need to move you into Romans 12:2. Transformation does not come from surrendering your hearts; it comes from surrendering your beliefs." Romans 12:2 says, "Be transformed by the renewing of your mind." Let me say it again, "transformation does not come from surrendering your heart; it comes from surrendering your beliefs." Transformation is seeing in our experience the manifestation of God's promises in and through us.

We found out that surrendering our beliefs is often more challenging than surrendering our hearts. God got very personal with us. He said, "Steve, can you surrender the belief that you are inferior to other leaders and that there is something uniquely wrong with you?" I said, "Lord, this feels so true. If it feels this true, doesn't that mean it is true?" He said, "No. Feelings do not validate truth; they just validate what you believe is true." He asked Wendy, "Can you surrender the belief that you are shy, inadequate, and cannot speak well in front of others?" She said, "But that's who I am." He said, "That's not who you are. That is just who you have become."

We realized that we were renewing our minds not with what God was saying but with our feelings and past experiences. We were believing lies instead of believing truth. John 8:32 says, "The truth will make you free." In every area of our lives where we believe truth, we get free, and in every area of our lives where we believe lies, we are not free. Truth empowers us, while lies disempower our lives and create an unnecessary limited experience. We get saved when we believe in Jesus; we get free when we believe like Jesus.

The battle is really between lies and truth. I am not a devil-focused Christian, but a Jesus and belief-focused believer. I don't discount the devil, but he is not our biggest problem. What I believe is my biggest problem. If I believe truth, I get free, and if I am free, it would seem I am not being hindered by the devil. Even to put on the full armor of God in Ephesians 6, we need to believe something to get those armor pieces on us. Ephesians 6:16 says "Above all, taking the shield of faith with which you will be able to quench all the fiery darts of the wicked one." This shield of good beliefs will cause us to be able to resist self-limiting lies and allow us to live in freedom.

So, how do we know if we're believing a lie? It is difficult to know because the nature of deception is that we don't know we are deceived. Once we know we are deceived, we are no longer deceived. So how do we know? Well, I received a surprising indicator in the early 1990s when I was reading a book by Francis Frangipane called *The Three Battlegrounds*. One of the Battlegrounds is the mind. I read, "Every area of your life that doesn't glisten with hope means you are believing a lie and that area is a stronghold of the devil in your life." I read that and instantly became discouraged. I felt this way because I really tried to find one area where I had glistening hope but could not. It was not a convenient season to start believing higher. I had many things in my life telling me that I was a failure. I had an unsuccessful car, a non-successful salary and bank account, my hair was starting to get unsuccessful, my church size was not successful, and my home was not successful. I said to the Lord, "How does this sound to you? When things start getting better in my life, I will start believing better. Is that okay with you?" And He said, "There has to come a time in your life where you start believing higher than what you're feeling and experiencing; it is called faith." Faith believes and then sees. We are not called to believe after we see something in our experience, but before.

After hearing the quote about glistening hope, I prayed a dumb prayer. "Lord, please show me every lie that I am believing." I should not have prayed that. I should have prayed, "Lord, show me 10% of the lies I'm believing." I got the revelation that almost everything I believed in my life was a lie and I was pastoring a church! I realized I had good doctrine but bad beliefs. We certainly need to believe good Bible doctrines, but that will not help us to be victorious if we are believing lies.

The Power of Hope

"Now may the God of hope fill you with all joy and peace in believing, that you may abound in hope by the power of the Holy Spirit" (Romans

15:13). The God of hope fills us **"in believing"**. Increasing hope is the evidence we are renewing our minds with truth, while decreasing hope is the evidence we are renewing our minds with lies.

"Every area of your life that does not glisten with hope means you are believing a lie and that area is a stronghold of the devil in your life." As I mentioned earlier, when I first read this Francis Frangipane quote in the 1990s, I became discouraged. I realized I had good Biblical doctrine but bad life beliefs. My life was changed when I stopped trusting any belief or conclusion that did not have hope attached to it.

Hope is the belief that the future will be better than the present and we have the power to help make it so. Hope is an overall, optimistic attitude about the future based on the goodness and promises of God. I believe after love, hope is the most powerful leadership and influential quality there is. Our hope level determines our influence level, and he who has the most hope has the most influence. Truly, it is very difficult to influence that which you do not have hope for.

In Ezekiel 37, when God asked Ezekiel, "Can these bones live?" He was basically asking, "Ezekiel, what do you think about this? What you think will determine what I can do. Do you believe these bones have a good future?" After Ezekiel responded with, "Oh Lord God, you know," God told Ezekiel to prophesy to the bones and tell them they were going to live. He didn't say, "Ezekiel, watch me prophesy and change this by myself." No, the Lord has to partner with someone who has hope to accomplish His will (by the way, these bones came to life and became a great army).

God is not afraid to show us how dry things are, as long as we do not get our beliefs out of their dryness. We live in a time where we see dry bones everywhere- dry morality bones, dry unity bones, dry leadership bones, dry family bones, dry freedom bones, dry church bones, and more. Yes, we are to do everything God has called us to do to keep bones from getting dry, but, ultimately, it does not matter how dry they get. What matters is whether we have renewed our minds enough to believe the bones can live.

We all have at least one area in our lives (a very dry area) that is screaming at us, "This really is hopeless! Things will never change! It is only going to get worse!" You are hearing this and so am I. Recently, I was battling for hope in an area of my life and could not seem to get over the heaviness I was feeling. So, I went to my wife, Wendy, for help. She asked me a powerful question. "Steve, what do you need to believe to have hope in this area of your life?" Bingo! That is the question. It led me to focus on the promises of God, my biblical identity, and to believe my past prayers were working (even if I did not see them working). As I did this, my hope increased. This question, "What do I need to believe to have hope?" will cause you to know that a right believing focus is more important than a right living focus. Let's explore that more.

Right Living or Right Believing?

Is it more important to preach about right living or right believing? The Old Testament answer was right living, but the New Testament answer is clearly right believing – and right believing actually creates right living: "Be transformed by the renewing of your mind" (Romans 12:2). When we are focused on *right living* we are focused on our own efforts to **"do"** righteous. When we are focused on *right believing,* we place our trust in the finished work of Jesus that He has **"made"** us righteous.

Abraham, an Old Covenant person, is held up to us as the example of how to live in the New Covenant. "For the promise to Abraham and his offspring that he would be heir of the world did not come through the law but through the righteousness of faith. For if it is the adherents of the law who are to be the heirs, faith is null and the promise is void. For the law brings wrath, but where there is no law there is no transgression" (Romans 4:13-15).

Unfortunately, many in the New Covenant start in faith but go back to an Old Covenant mindset of focusing more on performance than on beliefs. "O foolish Galatians! Who has bewitched you? . . . Let me ask you only this: Did you receive the Spirit by works of the law or by hearing with faith? Are you so foolish? Having begun by the Spirit, are you now being perfected by the flesh?" (Galatians 3:1-3). We are living in the flesh (placing our trust in the flesh) if we are focused more on what we are doing than what we are believing.

Do you know what the opposite of faith is? It is not fear, it is works. There are two ways to approach God – faith and works. One "works" while the other does not. Those who would preach and emphasize holiness and good conduct *apart* from a heavy diet of emphasizing that we are righteous by faith will actually increase sin in the people they are trying to influence positively. "Now the law came in to increase the trespass, but where sin increased, grace abounded all the more" (Romans 5:20).

Focusing on the finished work of Jesus in that He already made us righteous will cause us to access that grace to live righteously. When we teach the God side first (what He has already done), it makes the man side easy. When we preach and teach right believing, there is an enabling grace of God (the ability of God) released to do what we could not and cannot do on our own.

"You have become dull of hearing . . you need someone to teach you again the basic principles of the oracles of God. You need milk, not solid food, for everyone who lives on milk is unskilled in the word of righteousness" (Hebrews 5:11-13). One of the greatest skills we can have is to be skilled in the word of righteousness. This means we are relentless in our belief and confession that we are the righteousness of God in Christ Jesus (see 2 Corinthians 5:21) even when we sin (miss the mark of God's highest for us).

Again, if our preaching and teaching are mainly emphasizing right living, we are part of the problem. If we believe the moral decline in our countries will not be stopped unless we as the church go back to strongly preaching against behavioral sin, then we are a big part of causing behavioral sin. We may seemingly get positive results in the short-term, but preaching the law will ultimately only increase sin. What we focus on, we will have more of. If we focus on sin we will see more sin, we will empower sin.

If, however, our preaching and teaching emphasize right believing in Jesus, who He is, what He has done for us, we become a source of victory to those we minister to. Our words will cause people to walk in victory over sin. They'll receive grace (God's ability) to overcome areas that have held them captive for years! We become part of God's solution!

Before I go on, I want to clarify this: I hate sin and wrong living. I have seen the horrible effects of sinful choices on individuals, families, and nations. It grieves me to witness the devastation and pain caused by wrong living. I agree with those who proclaim God will heal our land if we as God's people humble ourselves, pray, and turn from our wicked ways (2 Chronicles 7:14), but we cannot turn from our wicked ways apart from radically believing we are righteous. There is no other way to do this.

Here is how we know we are staying in faith and are skilled in the word of righteousness. If we immediately think and proclaim we are the righteousness of God in Christ Jesus in the following situations, then I believe we are skilled in the word of righteousness:

1. When we sin (miss the mark)
2. When we see moral decline around us
3. When we are tempted to move into regret and "if only" thinking
4. When we are battling sickness
5. When we are tempted to do wrong

So what should we be preaching: right living or right believing? The answer is clear. Only when we have a solid foundation of emphasizing right believing can we effectively release the supernatural grace of God to enable people to live right. Then accountability, wisdom, and confrontation become tools of encouragement instead of weapons of condemnation. We become God's ministers of reconciliation (2 Cor 5:21).

This is a radical message, so let me share what I am not saying as I trumpet this vital teaching at this hour:

- I am not saying if you are abusing others, bringing hurt to others, or living recklessly you should not get help from skilled people to protect you and others from pain caused by your choices.
- I am not saying there is never a time for strong preaching to shake people out of compromise and complacency.

The most important place to use our faith is concerning our righteousness. "Seek first the kingdom of God and His righteousness" (not our righteousness) "and all these things will be added to you" (Matthew 6:33). Some might think that the most important place to use our faith is to access healing, provision, or for other answered prayers, but it is not. I dream about a day when we will have repentance meetings where people are crying at the altar because of not believing they are righteous or loved, and they are more concerned about this revelation than what they are doing. It will be exciting to see the fruit that results from this.

What Then Are We to Believe?

Now that we have stated that right believing is to be prioritized over right living, what are some of the most important beliefs we need to intentionally strengthen in our lives? We've already identified righteousness as a priority, but what else? What should we regularly renew our minds with?

Unquestionably, beliefs like Jesus is God and Jesus rose from the dead are to be at the forefront of our mind renewal, but what else? Here are twenty-five of my favorite and most transformational beliefs that I encourage people to meditate on and regularly say. They will create hope, dismantle negative strongholds, and cause transformation.

1. **The Adaptability Belief** – I will thrive no matter what happens. (Philippians 4:11-13)

2. **The Hope Belief** – I believe the future will be better than the present and I have the power to help make it so. (Romans 15:13; Jeremiah 29:4-11)

3. **The Faith Belief** – I am thankful that God's promises and my past prayers are working in my life, my family's lives, my circumstances, and my nation. (Hebrews 11:1)

4. **The Forgiveness Belief** – My intentional forgiveness creates well-being for others and for me. (Luke 23:34; Acts 7:60-8:1)

5. **The Long-Term Thinking Belief** – My beliefs and choices are leaving a positive legacy for generations to come. (Hebrews 11:20)

6. **The Joy and Laughter Belief** – I have strength and longevity because I consistently activate joy and laughter in my life. (Nehemiah 8:10; Proverbs 17:22)

7. **The Solutions Belief** – In every situation I face, I have many options, solutions, and divine ideas. There is always a solution. (1 Corinthians 10:13; James 1:5)

8. **The Beliefs About Others** – I see people according to their potential, not according to their past. (2 Corinthians 5:16; Judges 6:12)

9. **The Soul Prosperity Belief** – My response to something is almost always more important than the something. (3 John 2)

10. **The "Bottom-Lining" Belief** – Even if the worst happens, I will be okay. (Daniel 3:16-18)

11. **The Training Focus Belief** – My current challenges and frustrations are my training ground for the greater influence I will have in the future. (James 1:2-5; Romans 5:3-4; Psalm 119:71)

12. **The Peace Belief**– Peace is one of my strongest weapons in prayer. (Philippians 4:6-7; Romans 16:20)

13. **The Follow Through and Integrity Belief** – I make commitments with forethought, and I follow through on what I say I will do. (Matthew 5:37; Psalm 15:4b)

14. **The Imagination Belief**– I use my imagination to activate my faith. (2 Corinthians 4:18)

15. **The Identity Belief** – I am not who my past says I am; I am who God says I am.(2 Corinthians 5:17; Hebrews 10:14)

16. **The Staying Relational Belief** – I will not withdraw my heart from people who disappoint me or that I hear negative information about. (1 Corinthians 13:4-7; 1 Timothy 5:19) (This does not mean that at times we won't have boundaries in relationships.)

17. **The Forward Movement Belief** – My forward movement in life causes Red Seas to part. (Exodus 14:15-21; Philippians 3:13)

18. **The Courage Belief** – I am brave and run at my Goliaths. (1 Samuel 17:48)

19. **The Authenticity Belief** – My authenticity connects my heart to people and gives them hope. (Philippians 3:12; 1 Peter 5:5-6)

20. **The Unique Purpose Belief** – I understand my assignment and giftings, and I know what God's called me to do and not to do. (Romans 12:4-8; 1 Peter 4:10-11)

21. **The Decision-Making Belief** – I am a great decision maker and attach faith to every decision I make. (Romans 14:5; James 1:5)

22. **The Being Loved by God Belief** – I am unconditionally loved by God and worthy to receive love and blessings today. (1 John 4:19; Luke 15:20)

23. **The Valuing Process Belief** – I don't wait for perfection to celebrate myself and be joyful. (Philippians 3:12-14)

24. The Encouraging Others Belief – I radically encourage others daily. (Hebrews 10:24-25; Hebrews 3:13)

25. The Spiritual Laws Belief – I honor God's spiritual laws therefore I increase in favor, finance, health, and happiness. (Joshua 1:8; Psalm 1:2-3)

Why don't you do an experiment and declare all of these every day for a month? Many have done this and testified about the positive results and many have continued beyond the month because of the transformation the declarations brought.

Conclusion

"Lord, I believe; help my unbelief!"

"Jesus the author and finisher of our faith."

I am so thankful God is empowering, finishing, and helping us on our journey to be fully convinced in our most important beliefs. I am excited to see how He is going to do it in you and in me.

CHAPTER 3

Fully Convinced In Key Areas of Our Lives

In chapter one we talked about the epidemic of doubt, insecurity, and guilt concerning our decision-making and how we feel about ourselves. In this chapter, we will examine the importance of being fully convinced in key areas of our lives. Before we look at these areas, it is important to remember the normal pattern for the greatest beliefs in our lives is this: 1) it first sounds ridiculous, 2) then it sounds possible, 3) then it sounds probable, and, 4) finally, we are fully convinced.

This is a shorter chapter that is pretty meaty (especially the list of areas to be fully convinced in). I suggest you take time to meditate on this chapter's content and identify what you believe God is personally highlighting to you.

Let's look at some of these main areas where we are to become fully convinced. Each of them is an area where we will be tempted to live in doubt and limiting beliefs, but we can expect Jesus, as the author and finisher of our faith (Hebrews 12:2), to grow and finish our beliefs in each powerful area listed.

1. **God Loves Me Unconditionally** – When Jesus was baptized, He had an encounter and revelation we are all to experience: "And

suddenly a voice *came* from heaven, saying, 'This is My beloved Son, in whom I am well pleased'" (Matthew 3:17). Before Jesus did any ministry, He was anchored in God's love and approval. "Then Jesus was led up by the Spirit into the wilderness to be tempted by the devil. And when He had fasted forty days and forty nights, afterward He was hungry. Now when the tempter came to Him, he said, 'If You are the Son of God, command that these stones become bread'" (Matthew 4:1-3). Do you notice here that the word "beloved" is left out of the devil's temptation? He knows that if we continue to be fully convinced of God's love, we are basically untouchable to him because God's perfect love will defeat the fear in us (1 John 4:18) and take all limits off our lives (Ephesians 3:14-20). This love is to be experienced and felt daily. A parent does not tell his two-year-old child, "Now listen to me, I am going to tell you something once, and I need you to remember it for the rest of your life: "I love you." No, a good parent tells their child every day, "I love you!" If we are not hearing and experiencing our Heavenly Father's love every day, we may not be hearing from God as well as we think we are.

2. **Identity (Believing I Am Who God Says I Am)** – We cannot consistently do what we don't believe we are. Let me say this again: We cannot consistently do what we don't believe we are. The second most important question in life is "Who do I say I am?" (The first most important question is "Who do I say Jesus is?"). If we are waiting for outward evidence in our behaviors and emotions to determine our beliefs about ourselves, then we will have greater difficulty in improving our behaviors, experiences, and choices. We are to believe we are strong to experience consistent strength. We are to believe we are righteous to experience consistent righteousness. And we are to believe we are good decision-makers to experience good decision-making consistently.

3. **What We Believe is More Important Than What We Do** – The kingdom of God is not moved forward by good conduct; it is moved forward by good beliefs. Blessings in the Old Covenant were dependent on good behavior (works of the law), but New Covenant blessings are advanced by good beliefs (faith). We are called **believers**, and this should indicate what we ought to be prioritizing. Certainly, character and integrity are important, but to change what we do, we must first change what we believe. Romans 12:2 does not say, "Be transformed by trying harder." It says, "Be transformed by the renewing of your mind."

4. **God's Promises** – "By which have been given to us exceedingly great and precious promises, that through these you may be partakers of the divine nature" (2 Peter 1:4). Just as Abraham ultimately became fully convinced about what God had promised him and Sarah (even though it looked impossible - Romans 4:18-21), we too have been given grace to be fully convinced about what God has promised us.

5. **God's Rhema Word Promises** – Rhema words are specific promises that God has made real to us. Rhema is a Greek word translated "word" in the New Testament (e.g. Ephesians 6:17; Matthew 4:4; Romans 10:17). Abraham received a promise that his descendants would be too numerous to be numbered (Genesis 13:16). After more than twenty years, Abraham had an encounter with the Lord (Genesis 17) where this promise was turned into a Rhema word for him. In this encounter, God changed his name from Abram (Exalted Father) to Abraham (Father of a Multitude). Abraham began to speak this promise over his life as his true identity. Others would reinforce this when they said his name. Romans chapter four talks about this when it says, "God who gives life to the dead by calling those things that do not exist as though they did" (verse 17). This is

45

referring to Abraham. It goes on to say, "He was strengthened in faith, giving glory to God" (4:20). And then later in that chapter, it says he became "fully convinced that what He had promised He was also able to perform" (Romans 4:21). After this process, he became fully convinced of the Rhema word which he then experienced through the birth of Isaac.

6. **Our Past Prayers** – "Therefore I say to you, whatever things you ask when you pray, believe that you receive *them,* and you will have *them*" (Mark 11:24). "Now this is the confidence that we have in Him, that if we ask anything according to His will, He hears us. And if we know that He hears us, whatever we ask, we know that we have the petitions that we have asked of Him" (1 John 5:14-15). We are to believe we have received what we pray for at the moment we pray (not waiting to believe until we see it in our experience). Philippians 4:6 tells us to pray "with thanksgiving" when we are tempted to worry about something. It is this ongoing thanksgiving that leads us to be fully convinced that we have already received what we have prayed for and that we will see it in our experience.

7. **Our Season and Our Assignments in This Season** – "Of the sons of Issachar who had understanding of the times, to know what Israel ought to do..." (1 Chronicles 12:32). Just as in nature, there are different seasons in our lives, families, ministries, cities, and nations. As we understand this and perceive we also have different giftings, callings, and assignments, we recognize we are not going to prioritize the same things as other people. We will not be doing the same things that other people are doing. Our assignments will be different. Our seasons will be different. Certainly, we will be partnering with people in similar seasons to accomplish great things, but it is vital that we become fully convinced regarding what we are supposed to be doing

and what we are not supposed to be doing (or what we are supposed to be emphasizing in a particular season and what we are not supposed to be emphasizing). This is a key area to be fully convinced in.

8. **The Commitments We Have Made or Are Making** – "Each one must give as he has decided in his heart, not reluctantly or under compulsion, for God loves a cheerful giver" (2 Corinthians 9:7 ESV). Cheerfulness is a main indicator we have attached faith to our commitments and responsibilities. Doubt concerning these creates a "reluctantly or under compulsion" attitude which is the opposite of living a fully convinced lifestyle concerning our decisions, commitments, and responsibilities. Whether it is cleaning our house, paying a bill, being a parent, attending a meeting, or our job, a chronic lack of cheerfulness regarding things we are doing is a sign we are not fully convinced we should be doing them.

9. **Grace and the Finished Work of the Cross** – "For if by the one man's offense death reigned through the one, much more those who receive abundance of grace and of the gift of righteousness will reign in life through the One, Jesus Christ" (Romans 5:17). We cannot mix the works of the law with grace, but are to realize the importance of being fully convinced of the New Covenant message of grace and righteousness. In order to ground ourselves in New Covenant theology, I believe there are seventeen chapters in the Bible to immerse ourselves in. These chapters are to be the lens through which we interpret the rest of Scripture. They are Galatians chapters 1-6, Romans 4-8, Hebrews 4, Colossians 1-2, and Ephesians 1-3. All of these chapters are foundational if we are to be fully convinced that we are blessed because of what Jesus has done, not because of what we're doing.

47

10. **Non-Black-and-White Doctrinal Issues** – Romans 14:5 says, "One person esteems one day above another; another esteems every day alike. Let each be fully convinced in his own mind." Black-and-white issues are clearly revealed in Scripture (e.g. not murdering, not stealing, not committing adultery, etc.). There are unchanging truths in the Bible that need to be honored regardless of what the popular opinion is, but there are other areas where people may have different opinions about something and both be right. This is the implication of what is shared in Romans 14:5. One person is fully convinced the sabbath is a particular day, while another believes every day is the sabbath. Certainly, we need a good process in deciding what to believe about such matters (a process which is outlined in other parts of this book), but we cannot rise up to our full strength in the Lord without attaching faith to what we believe in areas where others believe differently. If we do not decide what we are going to believe, we will greatly limit our lives. Remember, a bad decision or belief made in faith has a greater likelihood of success than a good decision or belief made in doubt. And one final note here – the principles taught in this paragraph also apply to behavioral choices. Not everyone is going to have the same convictions on such things as nutrition, alcohol, media choices, etc. Our callings, assignments, and culture will influence these areas where we are not given a black-and-white directive from Scripture. And, it's also possible that we eventually may change our view.

11. **Focusing Primarily On What Is Right With Us, Rather Than What Is Wrong With Us** – "Likewise you also, reckon yourselves to be dead indeed to sin, but alive to God in Christ Jesus our Lord " (Romans 6:11). If we are primarily trying to fix our weaknesses instead of building on our strengths, we have a negative focus in our lives and will put a limitation on our potential. If

we have a tendency of going to bed regularly rehearsing and remembering our failures instead of our victories during the day, then we are sin-conscious instead of righteousness conscious. When we take communion, if we fixate on what is wrong with us instead of what Christ has done and thus what is right with us, we have an unhealthy habit that will work against us. Yes, if our lifestyle choices are hurting us and others, then we need to pursue accountability and help while we keep strengthening our beliefs, but know this; accountability is not an "account for my disabilities," but an account for my abilities (just as the Parable of the Talents teaches us Mattthew 25:14-30).

12. **Current Circumstances Are Training Us For Our Prophetic Destiny** – "Where there is no prophetic vision the people cast off restraint" (Proverbs 29:18 ESV). "Brethren, I do not count myself to have apprehended; but one thing I do, forgetting those things which are behind and reaching forward to those things which are ahead" (Philippians 3:13). Having a prophetic vision for our lives means we believe we are important in what God is doing, and we are being prepared for greater significance and influence in the future. Vision for the future gives power and purpose to the present because I know everything in my life now is training and preparation for my future prophetic destiny. This does not mean we devalue what we are doing now (nor does it mean we passively accept everything we experience as being sent by God), but this training mindset will help us see our frustrations and challenges as growth opportunities to become the person who can steward well the increase in the days ahead. "My brethren, count it all joy when you fall into various trials, knowing that the testing of your faith produces patience. But let patience have its perfect work, that you may be perfect and complete, lacking nothing" (James 1:2-4). When we

are fully convinced God is preparing us for greater things, we will embrace "all joy" concerning the various trials we may face.

13. **Forward Movement in Our Lives** –. One of my favorite declarations is, "My forward movement in life causes Red Seas to part." It comes from Exodus 14:15, "And the Lord said to Moses, 'Why do you cry to Me? Tell the children of Israel to go forward.'" The Children of Israel were stuck in a hard place. Their future was blocked (Red Sea) and their past was catching up to them (the Egyptians were pursuing them). In that situation, God said their priority was forward movement, not prayer. One of the greatest questions we can ask the Lord is this, "How can I move forward now?" or "What does forward movement look like in this area of my life?" This is a key for confident living, especially concerning areas of our lives that are difficult. Whether it be a relational, financial, or personal problem, as we are able to clarify the specifics for forward movement, this will insulate us from doubt, shame, and discouragement. The forward movement could be to trust our prayers are working, or it could be a specific step or steps regarding an issue. When we can say, "I believe God has said to do this" about a situation, we will much less likely be discouraged or drained by unresolved aspects of our lives.

14. **God's Will Is For Us To Live In Victory and Be Blessed** – "Now this is the confidence that we have in Him, that if we ask anything according to His will, He hears us. And if we know that He hears us, whatever we ask, we know that we have the petitions that we have asked of Him" (1 John 5:14-15). Faith begins where the will of God is known. How do we know what the will of God is for our lives? Here are some questions to ask which will help us discern it: 1) What was God's intention for us at creation? 2) What do we see as God's heart on a matter in the Bible as we study from Genesis to Revelation? 3) What curses did Jesus take for us on

the cross? 4) When Jesus instructed us to pray, "Your kingdom come. Your will be done on earth as it is in heaven," what curses are on earth that are not in heaven, and what blessings are in heaven that are not on earth? All of these questions will help us know God's will and help us pray and live in confidence.

15. **We Will Know What To Do** – "If any of you lacks wisdom, let him ask of God, who gives to all liberally and without reproach, and it will be given to him. But let him ask in faith, with no doubting, for he who doubts is like a wave of the sea driven and tossed by the wind" (James 1:5-6). "Let him ask in faith." These are powerful words. The instruction infers we can ask in doubt or as a religious duty prayer. If we ask in faith, we will also stay in faith after praying, believing that wisdom is coming. The fully convinced lifestyle includes continual thanksgiving and excitement about the wisdom that is flowing to us in the areas where we are unsure about what to do.

16. **We Will Have Favor With Those We Are Supposed To Have Favor With** – Favor is approval, support, or liking for someone or something. "And Jesus increased in wisdom and stature, and in favor with God and men" (Luke 2:52). My wife, Wendy, believes if someone is supposed to like her, they will; and if they are not important in God's plan for her future, then their favor is not important to pursue. This does not mean we do not consider habits and attitudes that may hinder favor in the eyes of others, but it does remove the pressure of feeling the need to try to impress people.

Which of the above are you the most convinced about? Which of them are you the least convinced about? Which belief do you believe is the most important for you to grow in now?

What Decisions or Commitments Do You Have Doubts About?

All of the above areas are important to be fully convinced about, but here, I want to give special focus to the decisions that we are making and have made. It is not uncommon for people to have doubts about decisions they've made or commitments that they have, but a lot of this is very subtle. Consider these areas where it is common to have struggled:

1. Financial commitments or expenditures
2. How to relate to family members

As we have said, cheerfulness is one of the signs we have attached faith to our decisions and commitments. "Each one must give as he has **decided** in his heart, not reluctantly or under compulsion, for God loves a cheerful giver" (2 Corinthian 9:7). The principle here is that God loves a cheerful decider. Even though financial giving is the focus of the chapter, this verse has keys for all the decisions we make.

God loves a cheerful giver (or cheerful decider). Why does He love this type of person? Let's explore this.

There are four main mindsets we can have concerning our commitments and decisions:

1. **Reluctance and Compulsion** - We are doing something but don't want to. This is called dead works, and repentance from dead works is the first elementary principle of Christ listed in Hebrews 6:1-2. **Doubt** - We are doing something but not sure we should be doing it.

2. **Passivity** - We follow through on a decision or commitment, but are emotionally neutral and waiting to see what happens.

3. **Faith** - We believe we are to be doing what we are doing, and we believe the result of this commitment will result in great fruit in the future.

Certainly, we could also do certain things in other ways than these four (e.g. rebellion, being controlled by another, etc.), but the mindsets listed here would be the most common for those reading this book.

Again, cheerfulness is evidence we are fully convinced (have attached faith to what we are doing). Joy is indeed a fruit of good beliefs. "Now may the God of hope fill you with all joy and peace in believing" (Romans 15:13). When we believe, our hope, joy, and peace increase. This is one reason God loves a cheerful decider. It is evidence of faith and "without faith it is impossible to please Him" (Hebrews 1:6).

If God loves a cheerful decider, then we can conclude He dislikes it when:

- We believe He does not trust us to make good decisions
- We think He is more interested in our obedience than our faith
- We believe that cheerfulness and gladness are unimportant or unattainable
- We do things out of compulsion or obligation

Before I move on, I want to clarify something about dead works. I am not saying that we should allow our feelings to be the deciding factor in what we do or don't do. We must all learn to keep commitments when we don't feel like keeping them. A main part of our growing into an integrous leader is our ability to follow through on our commitments even when we don't feel like following through. And the strength of our families (and ultimately our societies) is our ability to keep covenant commitments even when it is hard (consider the vows said at a marriage).

With that said, we cannot continually live in doubt or compulsion concerning the key areas of our lives. Doubt means we are not convinced we are doing the right thing. Compulsion means we are being forced to do something we really don't want to do (maybe feeling trapped by circumstances or by something we believe God wants us to do but we don't want to do it).

What are the most important aspects of your life where you are battling doubt and/or compulsion? What key areas have you not been a cheerful decider in? Is it your marriage? Is it how you should relate to your adult child? Is it whether you should stay in the church you are in? Is it whether you should date a particular person or become more intentional about finding a spouse? Is it about giving tithes and offerings? Is it whether you should stay at your current job? Is it a habit you have in your personal life? Or is it something else?

Take a moment to identify the most important commitments you have made where you do not have cheerfulness. What is the root problem concerning these? Is it doubt? Is it compulsion? Is it passivity?

Now implement the following decision-making model that will be taught in detail in the next chapter.

1. Clarify your options.
2. List under each option why it seems to be a good option and why it may not be a good option. This would include scripture, counsel from people you respect, and "God stories" (rhema words, dreams, prophetic words, unusual coincidences, etc.).
3. Ask in faith for wisdom (James 1:5-6). Delight yourself in God and how He is going to give you wisdom. Remember, the anxiety of

not knowing what to do is a bigger problem than not knowing what to do.

4. Identify new God stories and insights (dreams, prophetic words, etc.) and place these under each of your options.
5. Make a conclusion (Acts 16:10 NKJV) of what you believe you are to do and then attach faith to it. Affirm to yourself why this decision has long-lasting benefits to you and others.

You might ask, "But what if after I conclude, I begin to doubt or feel forced to do something?" When I have experienced this, I have had this conversation with the Lord. "Father, I have concluded I am to go in this direction. If you want to change my mind, then I need another God story from you. I refuse to change my mind based on negative emotions or circumstances." Of course, there will be times when we need to clarify our options again and make a different conclusion, but we cannot be tossed to and fro in our beliefs about what we are doing. Remember, how we make a decision is more important than the decision itself.

Let me proclaim this again: A bad decision made in faith has a greater likelihood of success than a good decision made in doubt. Fully convinced people know this and attack doubt and compulsion with what they believe God has said. "And take . . . the sword of the Spirit, which is the word of God" (Ephesians 6:17). We are to "kill" doubt, double mindedness, guilt, compulsion, and passivity with what we believe God has said.

Go . . . Doubting Nothing

Here is a great scriptural example of being fully convinced. It is a blog I wrote called, "Go . . . Doubting Nothing."

"Then the Spirit told me to **go with them, doubting nothing**. Moreover these six brethren accompanied me, and we entered the man's house" (Acts 11:12).

In Acts chapter 11, Peter tells the other Apostles why he fellowshipped with Gentiles and ministered to them as described in Acts 10. This was forbidden for Jewish people, and many were upset about it. "Now the apostles and brethren who were in Judea heard that the Gentiles had also received the word of God. And when Peter came up to Jerusalem, those of the circumcision contended with him, saying, 'You went into uncircumcised men and ate with them!'"

Peter shares the supernatural phenomenon he experienced (trance, vision, hearing a voice talking to him, etc.) that caused him to do something so risky. In the middle of his explanation, he says, "Then the Spirit told me to go with them, doubting nothing." I believe the phrase "Go . . . doubting nothing" is a "now word" for many reading this today.

"Doubting nothing" is another way of saying to attach faith to what we are doing and to be fully convinced. Let's look at two verses about being fully convinced (doubting nothing).

- "One person esteems *one* day above another; another esteems every day *alike*. **Let each be fully convinced in his own mind**" (Romans 14:5). We are to have a good process of decision-making, and then "doubt nothing" in our minds.
- "(Abraham) did not waver at the promise of God through unbelief, but was strengthened in faith, giving glory to God, and being **fully convinced** that what He had promised He was also able to perform" (Romans 4:20-21). We learn here that it is a process for us to become stronger in faith, and our faith goal concerning who we are is to be fully convinced (doubting nothing).

Another powerful verse on living doubt-free is in James 1. "If any of you lacks wisdom, let him ask of God . . . But let him ask in faith, with no doubting, for he who doubts is like a wave of the sea driven and tossed by the wind" (James 1:5-6). These verses are like the tracking number that we get when we order something to be delivered to our house. When I receive the tracking number, I immediately attach faith that what I ordered is coming. In the same way, when we ask for wisdom to know what to do, we are to go (after we pray) fully convinced we will know what to do.

One final verse: "**Being confident** of this very thing, that He who has begun a good work in you will complete it until the day of Jesus Christ" (Philippians 1:6). We can walk in a "doubting nothing" mindset that God will finish what He started in us, in our loved ones, and in our nations.

God has empowered us to be confident, fully convinced, and "doubting nothing" as we go, and move forward in life. Even if you have recently been battling insecurities and lacking confidence, I am confident that He who has begun a good work in you will keep on completing it until you go to your heavenly home.

Finally, the Spirit told Peter to go and doubt nothing regarding a new thing God was doing. Peter needed a big confirmation to break out of the old and into the new. There are people reading this who are grounded in the Word, and have been very faithful in their assignment, who are now going to embark on a new thing others may question. However, the confirmations are so big that it would take more faith to not do it than to do it. You are hearing the Spirit say to you, "Go and doubt nothing." There is a gift of faith manifesting in you as you go. And, I am hearing it will make a huge difference for the kingdom.

Conclusion

In this chapter, we have shared important areas where we are being empowered by God to be fully convinced. We have also taken inventory of commitments and responsibilities which we are not fully convinced about. In our next chapter, we will discuss the traits of great decision-makers. What we will learn will help us accelerate our movement toward a lifestyle of being fully convinced.

CHAPTER 4

The Art of Decision-Making

When we face a challenge or want to achieve a dream, there are two questions we need to ask ourselves:

1. What do I need to believe?
2. What do I need to do?

Both are vital to contemplate. Considering what to believe is the most important, but what we decide to do is obviously very important as well. This chapter focuses primarily on the question, "What do I need to do?" and how to determine that. Get ready to have your decision-making process strengthened in incredible ways.

7 Traits of Great Decision-Makers

The average adult makes 35,000 decisions every day. Most of these are minor issues like what cup of coffee to choose. Other choices are more important (e.g. where to live, major financial purchases, etc.). We even make decisions about what to believe concerning who we are and the significance of what we are doing. Decision-making is a big part of our lives. Even if we don't feel like we are successful in making decisions, the good news is we can develop greater skills in making the choices that lead to blessing and increase.

There are two extremes in the kinds of people who make decisions. The first are the impulsive, feeling-based decision-makers. They are passionate and wholehearted, but often do not consider the consequences of their choices because they are only concerned about experiencing happiness or rewards now. Certainly, there are positive aspects of being a quick decision-maker (consider Peter getting out of the boat and walking on water), but being a primarily feelings-based decider can create a lot of problems. On the other extreme is what I would call the perfectionist or religious mindset decision-makers. These are sincere people who walk in regular double-mindedness and doubt because of a haunting feeling that their decisions might be wrong, embarrassing, or displeasing to God. They have a fear of appearing flawed to others and often have a fear of punishment mindset in their relationship with God. Both of these extremes can be overcome, and this chapter will help you do so by strengthening your skill in making decisions.

Here is a powerful truth: **How we make decisions is ultimately more important than the decisions we make**. A good analogy for this is to consider a basketball player who wants to make more baskets. For them, it is more important to learn the mechanics of good shooting than it is to focus on making shots. If they keep shooting basketballs with poor technique, they will not be as effective in the game of basketball. The player who dedicates himself to practicing the fundamentals of good shooting will ultimately make more baskets. What a great analogy for decision-making. This chapter will help you understand what decision-making techniques to practice.

Great decision makers practice the following seven traits that we will go over in detail:

1. They base their decisions on the Bible and its core values.
2. They believe they are good decision-makers.
3. They know when not to make a decision.
4. They have hope for the future.
5. They include the right people in their decisions.
6. They clarify their options and have a story from God for what they conclude and decide to do.
7. They attach faith to the decisions they make.

Let's look at each of these traits in detail.

1. Great Decision-Makers Base Their Decisions on the Bible and Its Core Values

The Bible is the "owner's manual" for life. It is the book of wisdom. I have never followed God's clear direction and regretted it. Certainly, there can be short-term discomfort in choosing God's wisdom, but there is always a long-lasting blessing. Not following God's core values can produce pleasure for a season (Hebrews 11:25), but it creates long-lasting problems. The Book of Proverbs is a great place to start for understanding wisdom and God's core values for successful living.

Let me illustrate how it is obvious God's ways lead to blessing and are at the core of good choices. Imagine two people who are twenty years old. The first one completely ignores God's laws and is selfish, ungrateful, sexually promiscuous, a drunkard, prideful, slothful, jealous, unforgiving, lies, and hates God. The second loves God and is honest, humble, and generous, works hard, loves, keeps commitments, forgives, and prioritizes an intimate relationship with Jesus. What would you expect each to look like and be experiencing in thirty years? The one who chose to honor God would almost certainly be prospering in relationships, emotional well-being, and positive influence on society, while the other would likely be experiencing relational breakdowns, addictive behaviors, mental anguish, and be a negative influence on society.

I frequently say that what we believe is more important than what we do. This is true, but if our beliefs have not influenced our behaviors, then we do not actually believe what we think we believe. Right believing causes right living. The Apostle James says, "Faith without works is dead" (James 2:17). When we renew our minds according to Romans 12:2, we will see transformation in our emotions, our behavior, our abilities, our wisdom, and ultimately in our circumstances. Right believing is the root and right living is the fruit.

Joshua 1:8 is a great verse to illustrate this. "This Book of the Law shall not depart from your mouth, but you shall meditate in it day and night, that you may observe to do according to all that is written in it. For then you will make your way prosperous, and then you will have good success." As we prioritize God's truth through declarations and meditation, we will be propelled toward obedience ("observing to do according to all that is written in the law"), and then onto success and prosperity.

2. Great Decision-Makers Believe They Are Good Decision-Makers

We cannot consistently do what we don't believe we are. The Bible says we have the mind of Christ (1 Corinthians 2:16), and I can safely say that means we have the DNA of a great and healthy person in decision-making. The nature of faith is that we believe before we see. As we declare things like "I always know what to do and have incredible grace to follow through," we will build the identity needed for life-launching decisions.

There are two main ways we "work" to see improvement in an area of our lives. The first is to invest in our identity beliefs, and the second is to practice. For instance, if you want to grow as a public speaker, you need to first develop a plan to strengthen your beliefs that you are a good speaker. Then you study how to effectively speak, take every opportunity you can to speak, and receive feedback on ways you can improve. Practicing a skill is important, but it is not as important as believing you have the skill.

"Be transformed by the renewing of your mind" (Romans 12:2). Because there is no limit to how much we can renew our minds, there is no limit to how much we can be transformed. As we consider decision-making, this truth is exciting. The content of this book is designed to help you become fully convinced in many areas, but one of the most important is this belief: you are a great decision-maker who always knows what to do. This truth alone is worth the whole book.

3. Great Decision-Makers Know When Not To Make a Decision

We are powerful people growing in faith-filled decision-making, but there are times in life when we should not trust our thinking. Here are ten times when it is very unwise to make substantial decisions or come to any major conclusions.

- **When We Are Tired** - "But Elijah himself went a day's journey into the wilderness and came and sat down under a broom tree. And he asked that he might die, saying, 'It is enough; now, O Lord, take away my life, for I am no better than my fathers'" (I Kings 19:4). When we are tired, things can look much worse than they really are. Once Elijah rested, he had a better perspective. Sometimes one of the best things we can do for ourselves is to just take a nap.

- **When We Are Angry** - "Know this, my beloved brothers: let every person be quick to hear, slow to speak, slow to anger; for the anger of man does not produce the righteousness of God" (James 1:19-20). There are times when righteous anger works for us, but the "anger of man" has caused many harmful decisions and conclusions to be made. It is a wise person who says, "I need to walk away from this now so I don't say or do something stupid."

- **When Our Primary Relational Connections Are With the Wrong People** - "Whoever walks with the wise becomes wise, but the companion of fools will suffer harm" (Proverbs 13:20). The people we allow into our inner circle will dramatically affect our thinking and choices. This does not only include our relationships but also the media we "fellowship" with. If "faith comes by hearing" (Romans 10:17), what and who we listen to actually counsel us, whether we're aware of it or not. I recommend Danny Silk's ministry, Keep Your Love On, as a powerful resource to improve the quality of our relationships.

- **When We Are Lonely** - "But if we walk in the light, as he is in the light, we have fellowship with one another, and the blood of Jesus his Son cleanses us from all sin" (1 John 1:7). Isolation creates delusional thinking. Elijah succumbed to this in 1 Kings 19. The psalmist in Psalm 73 also battled lies, even becoming envious of the ungodly. The deception stayed with him until "one day he was brought into the sanctuaries of God and in the light of his glory, his distorted perspective vanished" (Psalm 73:17 TPT).

- **When We Are Disconnected From God** - "But the fruit of the Spirit is love, joy, peace, patience, kindness, goodness, faithfulness, gentleness, self-control; against such things there is no law" (Galatians 5:22-23). This fruit will cause us to make good decisions and conclusions. These attributes are not those we work on, but they result from a life-giving connection with God. He is the true vine, and any good fruit will come out of our abiding in Him (John 15:5). If we try to change our behavior without addressing our relationship with God, then we miss the most important component of victorious living.

- **When We Are Prideful** – "Peter answered him, 'Though they all fall away because of you, I will never fall away'" (Matthew 26:33). Peter's pride cut him off from God's empowering grace. "God opposes the proud but gives grace to the humble" (James 4:6). Pride is an enemy of good decision-making and good conclusions. When we believe we are better than other people, when we believe our success is the result of our good works, and when we don't think we need to spend time in prayer and the Bible, pride has infiltrated our thinking and will keep us from seeing clearly.

- **When We Are Emotional or Not Feeling Well** – "Hope deferred makes the heart sick, but w*hen* the desire comes, *it is* a tree of life" (Proverbs 13:12). Whether it is that time of the month, an emotional funk, or fighting off a sickness, we all have times where we cannot trust the perspective we have. The Bible frequently uses the phrase, "And it came to pass." I am glad it does not say, "And it came to stay." Often the best thing we can do is say to ourselves, "I am going to wait a few days before deciding or concluding about big things in my life."

- **When Facing a Mob Mentality** - "And all the people of Israel grumbled against Moses and Aaron. The whole congregation said to them, 'Would that we had died in the land of Egypt! Or would that we had died in this wilderness!'" (Numbers 14:2).

Sometimes we find ourselves in groups that are offended or lash out in judgment in an attempt to solve a problem. This can happen when we are physically with people or in social media settings. Either way, it is dangerous to allow the offenses of others to sweep us into hasty conclusions and decisions which are contrary to our core values. Stepping away from the heightened emotions of the moment will bring much-needed clarity.

- **When We Are Overly Concerned About What People Think About Us** - "Now when Peter had come to Antioch, I withstood him to his face, because he was to be blamed; for before certain men came from James, he would eat with the Gentiles; but when they came, he withdrew and separated himself, fearing those who were of the circumcision. And the rest of the Jews also played the hypocrite with him, so that even Barnabas was carried away with their hypocrisy" (Galatians 2:11-13). People pleasing and "the fear of man" will greatly hinder quality decisions.

- **When We Are Disappointed** - "Let us hold fast the confession of our hope without wavering, for He who promised is faithful" (Hebrews 10:23). Hope is the safety net when what we believe for in faith does not happen. Those who do not have hope as the foundation for their faith will have a very difficult time overcoming disappointment. This is because they will tend to believe they cannot live fully unless they are experiencing what they are believing for. Hope people believe they will thrive no matter what happens and this is a key to overcoming disappointment. If we stay disappointed, we will be prone to make decisions to isolate, self-medicate, and escape from responsibility. The next trait of great decision-makers will explain this more.

Successful people find ways to protect themselves from doing or saying dumb things when they are not doing well (especially when not doing well emotionally). They largely do this by having relationships with people they trust (family, friends, leaders, etc.) who they have invited to speak wisdom and even confront them if they are seen to be headed in the wrong direction. With that said, let's now explore how hope leads to great decision-making.

4. Great Decision-Makers Have Hope For the Future

"Where there is no prophetic vision the people cast off restraint" (Proverbs 29:18). Prophetic vision is linked to hope, and hope is the belief that the future will be better than the present, and we have the power to help make it so. Without vision and hope, "the people cast off restraint." In other words, they believe there is nothing to live for, therefore their decision-making is reduced to just trying to survive and be happy now. On the contrary, those who believe there is hope and that things will get better will make higher choices to invest in a better future.

Viktor Frankl in his book, *Man's Search for Meaning*, recounts how hope for the future was the single most important factor in determining whether his fellow prisoners survived the Nazi concentration camps in World War II or not. He wrote, "The prisoner who had lost faith in the future - his future - was doomed. With his loss of belief in the future, he also lost his spiritual hold. He let himself decline and become subject to mental and physical decay." The lack of hope reduced the type of decisions to its lowest form (the avoidance of pain).

Frankl, who helped millions value hope after he was released from the concentration camps, had at the core of his therapy this truth: human beings are driven by their views of their own future. The more positive the future is seen, the more power and purpose there will be for the present to make decisions to benefit themselves and society.

"Without a vision the people perish" (Proverbs 29:18). A lack of clear purpose for the future will not only drain us of energy now but will actually shorten our lives. During the American Revolution, the average life span was less than forty years, but most of our nation's founding fathers lived at least twenty years longer. It would seem their vision to create a great nation literally gave them life.

Frankl had a "why" to live for as a prisoner. His "why" was that he wanted to see his family again, and he wanted to write his book. This vision caused him to decide to endure intense suffering by seeing it as something that would make him stronger for his future.

When we don't have a "why" to live for, we are reduced to trying to protect what we have, focusing on the past, and we will only change to avoid pain. Our purpose will be reduced to trying not to lose what we have left (trying not to move backward in life). This was Gideon's mindset in Judges 6 when an angel told him while he was in a winepress hiding and threshing wheat, "The Lord is with you, mighty warrior" (Judges 6:12). His "why" was survival, not to try and make things better. When we lose hope, we stop investing and improving.

Again, hope is the belief that the future will be better than the present and we have the power to help make it so. When we don't have this strong vision and purpose for the future, we will live from our past instead of our future. Our thinking will fixate on the past (regrets, good old days, if only, etc.), and, as a result, we will adopt a victim mindset and be without vitality in the present.

"One thing I do: forgetting those things that are behind and reaching forward to those things that are ahead" (Philippians 3:13). There are "those things" for all of us to reach forward to. Clarifying what "those things" are is a main part of living in hope.

Why are you alive? What difference do you want to make in the future? What problem do you want to fix? What strength do you want to bring to your family or society? These are the questions that hope ignites in us.

I believe all of heaven gets behind people who make hope-filled decisions to invest in a better future. As I think of this, the biblical character, Nehemiah, comes to mind. He had a "secular" job (king's cupbearer), and he heard the walls of Jerusalem were broken down. He said, "I am going to do something about that! I am a person of hope who believes things will get better, and I have the power to help make it so." After he decided to do this, incredible resources and favor followed his choice. We too will have heaven's resources manifest when we decide to fix and improve things like:

- Disconnection in our families
- Anxiety
- Homelessness
- A lack of joy and hope in God's people (I've specifically chosen that one)
- Racial divisions

Once we get hope for the future (having a purpose and the belief we can make a difference), we will be amazed at the multiple options we will see for reaching our goals. In his book, *Be Your Future Self Now,* Dr. Benjamin Hardy quotes Dr. Charles Snyder, whom Hardy says is the world's leading expert and researcher on hope. Snyder says, "High hope people find multiple pathways to reach their goals and willingly try new approaches to do so. Low hope people, on the other hand, stick with one approach and do not try other avenues. If stymied, Instead of using problem-focused thoughts, the low hope people often use counterproductive avoidance and disengagement thinking. Reinforced in the short-term by their avoidance thoughts, low hope people will continue their passivity. Unfortunately, they do not learn from past experiences. High hope people, however, use information about not reaching their goals as diagnostic feedback to search for other feasible approaches."

High-hope people create a way because to have hope, you either see a way to realize your goal or are flexible enough to create a way. When hope exists, there is always a way to choose. There are no hopeless situations, just people who do not have hope. There is always a solution. Hope does not consider how bad the odds look for success but believes a difference can be made.

Napoleon said, "Leaders are brokers of hope". The difference between a leader and a manager is that the leader focuses on why the organization or group exists, while the manager focuses on efficiency. We need efficiency, but even that will break down without hope. Leaders make higher decisions than those who are simply trying to effectively manage their lives, families, or organizations.

Viktor Frankl had an understanding of the power of hope before he became a prisoner, but his hope was tested in the fire of adversity and therefore, what he says carries much weight. He said, "Human beings are driven by their views of their own future". Our decisions indeed are greatly influenced by the level of hope we have for the future.

5. Great Decision-Makers Include the Right People In Their Decision Making

"There is wisdom in a multitude of counselors" (Proverbs 15:22). "He who walks with the wise will be wise" (Proverbs 13:20). Our choice of friends and who we allow to influence us will dramatically affect the types of decisions we make. If we only hang out with turkeys, we will make turkey decisions. If we are connected with eagles who have a track record of making wise choices, then we will be much more prone to making very good choices. These people indirectly and directly influence our decisions depending on how close we are to them.

Good decision-makers pursue good people in their lives. It is one of the most important factors we will delve into in chapter six, "Empowered Toward Great Decisions". In this chapter, I want to introduce seven people we need in our lives. We definitely need a variety of people to help us go to the highest level. Wendy and I sure found this out.

After Wendy and I got married, we began to realize we could not meet all the needs in each other's lives. This was disappointing at first, but then we began to focus more on the strengths we each brought into the relationship rather than blaming the other for the needs he or she was unable to meet.

In truth, we can't meet every need for anyone in our lives. Each year I mentor a new team and tell them, "You will have a successful relationship with me if you can figure out what I bring to you and what I probably won't bring to you. I will be a spiritual father in your life, but I cannot be your only spiritual parent. I encourage you to maintain or pursue relationships with others to meet the needs I am not meeting."

The only singular source we have—God himself—has ordained for us to have five different types of ministry voices influencing us. "And He Himself gave some to be apostles, some prophets, some evangelists, and some pastors and teachers, for the equipping of the saints for the work of ministry, for the edifying of the body of Christ" (Ephesians 4:11-12). It is wise for us to allow each of these expressions to speak into our lives and help shape us. Bethel Church in Redding, CA (where I am on staff), is committed to seeing the "five-fold" leadership model be implemented and exported. This model is meant to ensure that we're encouraged *and* evangelized, challenged *and* instructed. This balance of ministry contributes to the health of the body of Christ.

We also need a variety of personal influences and input in order to be individually well-rounded and successful as we grow. No one person can provide the necessary perspective for all situations. Christ did not give us merely one part but a whole body (1 Corinthians 12:12-27). Each friend, confidant, or counselor will have something unique to contribute.

What Kinds of Voices Do We Need in Our Lives?

The Encouragers and Cheerleaders - They bring hope. They inspire us to overcome. They can be irritating at times because they don't seem to empathize at the highest level, but they are needed to spark and spur us on.

- "You can do this! This is a season of breakthrough for you."
- "God is going to make a way where there seems to be no way."
- "Here's a testimony of someone who has overcome what you are facing."
- "I think you should listen to Joel Osteen or Steve Backlund every day!"
- "God's promises are true."

The Challengers - They see where we are compromising or tolerating mediocrity. They are not always fun to experience, but we need their tough love to shake up our stagnation and complacency:

- "What are you doing?"
- "Where is this coming from?"

- "I don't understand."
- "I disagree with what you are doing or thinking."
- "You are better than this."
- "Stop compromising in your behaviors and thoughts.
- "Surrender everything to God!"

The Listeners and Empathizers - They give us the opportunity to process without judgment, without telling us what to do, and they are able to pull out of us the answers and courage to move forward. It is important however that these be forward-moving people who are not chronically stuck in their own defeat and victim mindsets.

- "Tell me what is really going on?"
- "I am so sorry."
- "That sounds so painful. I feel for you"
- "I stayed up all last night and prayed for you."
- "Tell me more about how you are feeling."

The Historians – These are trusted long-term friends and family members, people who are constant throughout the seasons of life. They can remind us of who we are when the pressure's on.

- "Look at how far you've come."
- "Remember when God came through for you last time? He'll do it again."
- "See how the pieces of your story are being woven together? God is doing a mighty work in you. You can stay the course to the finish line."
- "I believe in you."

The Improvers and Visionaries – These can be counselors, coaches, consultants, and idea people. They help us strategize, pinpoint fears that hold us back, and ask great questions to get us going.

- "Here are three ways we can do that better."
- "What could be possible if you weren't limited by this obstacle?"
- "What if there was a better solution?"
- "Have you considered something like this?"

The Students – As Michael Brodeur says, "Jesus did not say, 'Go into all the world and make good Sunday church meetings.' No, He said to go and make disciples" (Matthew 28). We need people to disciple and mentor. The body of Christ is a family, and we need younger brothers and sisters and sons and daughters to bring with us. As we contribute to the growth and development of others, we not only find a needed outlet for our generosity and hard-earned wisdom, but we also learn from those we encourage and include. Here are some things our students could say:

- "What you shared brought a lot of clarity to my process."
- "Thank you for the insights you gave, they helped me make a decision about my future."
- "In your experience, what has been the most impactful in shaping your leadership style?"
- "If you could go back in time, what key advice would you give your younger self?"

The Mentors – Someone who has successfully done what we are doing or want to do. As Joshua learned from Moses and Elisha followed Elijah, we can follow the example of mothers and fathers who are blazing trails ahead of us. Though no one is a copy of anyone else, we can learn invaluable lessons and receive priceless impartations as we humble ourselves to honor, serve, and learn from those who've gone before us. We will hear these types of insights from mentors:

- "When I faced a similar situation these are some of the things I did."

- "Have you considered speaking to so and so about this? They have overcome in this area."
- "Thank you for allowing me to speak into your life from my own journey."
- "It's good that you want to learn how I navigated this situation, it'll help you as you step into what's next."

"And my God shall supply all your needs" (Philippians 4:19). When we know what we need and then believe for it, the provision will come to us. It may be through someone we don't know personally (i.e. through a podcast, course, book, etc.), but God will provide the right people to inspire, encourage, challenge, remind, listen to, learn from, and shape us precisely when we need it.

These voices can come in many forms at different times in our lives. And the exciting thing is we get to be one or more of these in the lives of those around us.

There are certainly other types of people to positively influence us as we progress, but these seven will bring health and increase into our lives and our assignments over and over again. These relationships are worth searching out and investing in. They will help us to make higher-level decisions causing us to fulfill God's highest purpose for our lives. What they say will provide especially important input to us after we have clarified our options in what to believe or do when we are in the process of making a decision. These voices are not the only thing we list under our decision-making options, so let's look a little deeper at the concept of clarifying our options.

6. Great Decision-Makers Clarify Their Options and Have a Story From God For What They Conclude and Decide To Do

Many are in doubt and frustrated because they have not clarified their options about what to believe or do about a particular situation. When we take the step of listing the different directions we can take concerning a matter, we start empowering ourselves and creating forward movement concerning that situation. This technique is not only important as we face problems or challenges, but it is also vital for us as we move forward into possessing the dreams that are in our hearts. Once we list the different directions we can take concerning a matter, we will find clarity increasing. And when we take the next step of putting all the logical reasons why each option is a good direction or not, then our momentum and confidence will increase even more.

Yes, we may experience times where there seems to be no good option, but that is when we go back to strengthen the core beliefs discussed in chapter two:

- Adaptability – I will thrive no matter what happens.
- Solutions – In every situation I face, I have many options, solutions, and divine ideas. There is always a solution.
- Bottom-lining – Even if the worst happens, I will be okay.
- Forward Movement – My forward movement in life causes Red Seas to part.
- Courage – I am brave and run at my Goliaths.

These beliefs help us deal with anxiety and hopelessness as we move toward concluding what we are to do. It is important to get peace by believing these truths before we seek to conclude what to do.

After we have clarified our options, we can list the following under each option:

- Why it seems to be a good option
- Why it seems to be a poor option
- What key people have said
- What scripture says
- What are the "God stories" related to the option?

Next, we implement James 1:5-8. "If any of you lacks wisdom, let him ask God, who gives generously to all without reproach, and it will be given him. But let him ask in faith, with no doubting, for the one who doubts is like a wave of the sea that is driven and tossed by the wind. For that person must not suppose that he will receive anything from the Lord; he is a double-minded man, unstable in all his ways."

- We ask God for wisdom in faith.
- We stir up our thanksgiving and delight in the Lord as we excitedly anticipate the clarity that is coming.
- We add to our options the wisdom that comes (the opinions of key people, new scriptural insights, God stories, etc.)

God Stories

"Show me a sign of your favor" (Psalm 86:17 ESV).

After we have clarified our options in our decision-making process, we start putting in the God stories (unusual coincidences, dreams, prophetic words, visions, highlighted Bible verses, etc.) under the options. Remember, the greater the risk we take; the greater the story we need from God. To help in this, here are some examples of God stories in the Bible. (I will only go into detail about Gideon, but the rest will give you greater insight as you meditate on them). If God was trying to discourage these Bible heroes from the direction they ultimately took, then He did a bad job in doing so.

1. **Gideon and the Fleece in Judges 6** - Gideon asked God for a supernatural sign that helped push him over the top causing him to be fully convinced that he was called and capable of carrying out his big assignment to deliver Israel from bondage. "So Gideon said to God, 'If You will save Israel by my hand as You have said— look, I shall put a fleece of wool on the threshing floor; if there is dew on the fleece only, and it is dry on all the ground, then I shall know that You will save Israel by my hand, as You have said.' And it was so. When he rose early the next morning and squeezed the fleece together, he wrung the dew out of the fleece, a bowlful of water. Then Gideon said to God, 'Do not be angry with me, but let me speak just once more: Let me test, I pray, just once more with the fleece; let it now be dry only on the fleece, but on all the ground let there be dew. And God did so that night. It was dry on the fleece only, but there was dew on all the ground" (Judges 6:36-40). This is the classic God story in the Bible that created the concept of laying out a fleece in decision making. I will briefly mention a few more.

2. **Peter's Vision in Acts 10** - It caused him to do something that was a cultural taboo.

3. **Apostles Cast Lots in Acts 1** - This seemingly unusual way to decide (which is referred to numerous times in the Old Testament) was used to determine who would replace Judas.

4. **Abram's Encounter in Genesis 17** - This encounter was instrumental in Abraham becoming fully convinced.

5. **Joseph's Vivid Dreams as a Young Man in Genesis 37** - These dreams were so strong that they caused him to overcome betrayal, false accusation leading to prison, and being forgotten.

6. **Earthquake in the Prayer Meeting in Acts 4** - This sign and wonder caused the disciples to believe they were backed by heaven in what they were doing.

7. **Abraham's Servant's "Fleece" in Finding a Wife for Isaac in Genesis 24** - An amazing story of asking God for a sign.

8. **Mary's Visit From the Angel Gabriel in Luke 1** - An angelic visitation enabled Mary to embrace a situation that caused derision and great questions about her character.

9. **An Angel Appears to Joseph in a Dream in Matthew 1** - Joseph's dream caused him to make the illogical decision to stay with Mary.

10. **Ananias and Saul's Visions in Acts 9** - Two men's decision-making was altered by supernatural visions.

11. **Moses and the Burning Bush in Exodus 3** - A disappointed older leader was launched into nation-altering leadership through an encounter in the wilderness.

12. **Ruth's Unexpected Favor at Boaz's Field in Ruth 2** - This favor caused her to believe higher and experience higher in her life.

13. **Samuel's Call in 1 Samuel 3** - Samuel heard the audible voice of God and it helped him choose to believe he was significant.

Our internal peace, or lack of it, is also often a great indicator of God's leading. "And let the peace of God rule in your hearts" (Colossians 3:15). Could this be what happened to Paul in Acts 16? "Now when they had gone through Phrygia and the region of Galatia, they were forbidden by the Holy Spirit to preach the word in Asia. After they had come to Mysia, they tried to go into Bithynia, but the Spirit did not permit them" (vs 6-7). I have had different situations where God used a lack of peace (a "check" in my spirit) as a big part of my decision-making process.

Wisdom in Asking God for a Supernatural Sign to Determine His Will

It is important to understand that a fleece (sign from God) is only one part of the decision-making process. Without proper safeguards, people can use fleeces to "confirm" almost anything is from God. Even so, our God story (or fleece) is an incredible piece in becoming fully convinced in our identity and what we are to do. God stories help us to reach a conclusion regarding what option we are to choose as we conclude God is speaking to us and leading us in a particular direction.

Concluding Which Option to Take

When people say, "God told me this," or "God has led me to do that," it is almost always a conclusion that is being made, rather than them actually hearing an audible voice from God. It is a conclusion based on prayer, meditating on scripture, listening to Holy Spirit, and fellowshipping with others around the Word of God.

We gain much clarity on this as we consider how the Apostle Paul concluded he was to go to Macedonia. "Now when they had gone through Phrygia and the region of Galatia, they were forbidden by the Holy Spirit to preach the word in Asia. After they had come to Mysia, they tried to go into Bithynia, but the Spirit did not permit them. So passing by Mysia, they came down to Troas. And a vision appeared to Paul in the night. A man of Macedonia stood and pleaded with him, saying, 'Come over to Macedonia and help us.' Now after he had seen the vision, immediately we sought to go to Macedonia, **concluding** that the Lord had called us to preach the gospel to them" (Acts 16:6-10). Paul faced closed doors concerning what he was trying to do, but because of a vision, he concluded he was to go to Macedonia.

Again, almost every time we say, "God told me to do this," it is a conclusion we have made that we attach faith to. Certainly, the Word of God is very clear on many things about what to do and not do. In such matters, we can confidently say, "God has told me" to do something or not to do something. But in things that are not clear, such as who to marry, where to live, how significant we believe we are, what car to buy, or how to respond to a relationship difficulty, we make conclusions. And when we have a good process of decision-making like the one described above, we will be fully convinced about our conclusions and what we decide to do.

7. Great Decision-Makers Attach Faith to the Conclusions They Make

Once we have concluded what option to choose, we attach our faith to that choice. Romans 14:5 says "One person esteems one day above another; another esteems every day alike. Let each be fully convinced in his own mind." Once we have gone through a good process in making a decision, then we attach faith to the decision. In my relationship with God, I tell him that He can change my mind through another God story, but until He does, I am going to move forward being fully convinced with what I have concluded. As I have said, all of heaven gets behind people who attach faith to their decisions.

In the next chapter, we will go in-depth on what it means to attach faith to our decisions and beliefs. We will discuss when it is appropriate to change our minds concerning what we have concluded to do.

Conclusion

How we make decisions is more important than the decisions we make. Great decision-making is a skill we can develop. The truths shared in this chapter have served me well, and I believe will serve you well too.

CHAPTER 5

Attaching Great Faith to Everything We Do

Here are four of my favorite quotes to introduce this chapter.

1. "Steve, instead of waiting to do something great, why don't you attach great faith to what you are doing now and it will become great."

2. Faithfulness is not just showing up, it is how you think when you show up. You show up full of faith.

3. Three signs we have attached faith to our commitments and responsibilities are:
   - Energy
   - Cheerfulness
   - Power

4. *Declarations are a main way to attach great faith to who we are and what we do.*

The above four statements give a good indication of where we are going in this chapter. This section of the book will inspire you and give you a major ingredient in how to thrive and love life.

"He who would love life and see good days, let him refrain his tongue from evil, and his lips from speaking deceit" (1 Peter 3:10). There is a difference between loving God and loving life. Many believers love God but don't love life. This chapter will help change that. Let's start by looking again at 2 Corinthians 9:7.

God Loves a Cheerful Decider

2 Corinthians 9 is a strong chapter about the attitudes and benefits of financial giving. It reveals incredible promises. We will:

- Reap generously if we sow generously
- Have all grace abounding to us
- Experience all-sufficiency
- Be enriched in every way to be generous in every way

Although there are many great promises in this chapter, let's focus on verse seven which speaks directly to this book's theme of being fully convinced.

"Each one must give as he has decided in his heart, not reluctantly or under compulsion, for God loves a cheerful giver" (2 Corinthians 9:7).

Let's break this verse down phrase by phrase:

- **Each one** – Each person is free to decide what they do and do not do. Although the Bible does give clear direction on many issues, there are also issues not clear cut that we must decide on. In these cases, we must respect the decision-making and choices of others that are different from our own.

- **Must give as he has decided in his heart** – Again, we get to decide how much to give in finances, time, energy, and

84

relationships. This is an incredible revelation as we move from a slave mentality to a son mentality. Slaves are always waiting for a command from God or from others to know what to do, but sons are given increasing authority to decide for themselves through good decision-making processes. Our good Father models excellent decision-making for us, then gives us room to try for ourselves. He enthusiastically celebrates when we choose well!

- **Not reluctantly or under compulsion** – If we have either one of these attitudes towards what we give ourselves to, they reveal one of two problems - we are either doing the wrong thing or we are doing the right thing with the wrong beliefs. "Therefore let us leave the elementary doctrine of Christ and go on to maturity, not laying again a foundation of **repentance from dead works** and of faith toward God" (Hebrews 6:1). A dead work is Christian "obedience" done consistently in a reluctant manner or under compulsion. Repentance from this is one of the elementary doctrines of Christ.

- **For God loves a cheerful giver** – The Greek word for cheerful is *hilaros*, from which we get our word hilarious (boisterous merriment). Cheerfulness is evidence we have attached faith to our decisions. God loves a cheerful giver because that kind of person gives from their heart in faith. As they give, they think, "This is exciting. I have decided to do this. This is going to have a huge positive impact on me and others." Note: many churches do offering readings before the offering to stir up this cheerfulness.

Again, the principles of 2 Corinthians 9:7 are applicable far beyond finances, and we can rightly conclude that God loves a cheerful decider. **A chronic lack of cheerfulness in our disciplines, schedules,**

or responsibilities is most likely a sign we have decided out of obligation instead of faith. If this has happened to you, or you are currently living without consistent joy about your life and choices, then I suggest doing this:

1. **Clarify Your Options and Conclude What You Are To Do** – This is the key to living in faith concerning what we have decided to do.

2. **Speak Life Over Your Commitments** – "My meetings today are going to be powerful," or "God is going to show up in my family tonight when I get home," or "This coffee date with my friend will cause a breakthrough for both of us."

3. **Press Into Your Beliefs Until Cheerfulness Manifests Consistently Regarding the Choices You Have Made** – This may take a while, but the journey is incredible as we go deeper in defeating the lies that create a lack of cheerfulness in giving our time, finances, and energy.

God loves a cheerful decider because it is a major sign of spiritual maturity. Our Heavenly Father, as with any parent, loves it when His kids move from indecision to confidence in what they decide to do. 2 Corinthians 9:7 is a great verse to meditate on for the one who desires to be fully convinced. When we add the truths of Romans 14 to it, we gain even more understanding of the importance of attaching faith to what we decide to do.

The Romans 14 Gold Mine

Romans 14 is an incredible chapter for those who want to be fully convinced and attach faith to their actions. It speaks about personal responsibility, diversity in decision-making, deciding in faith, not negatively influencing those weaker in faith, and warns us about judging the choices of others. Here are some of the key phrases in the chapter:

- **"Receive one who is weak in the faith, but not to dispute over doubtful things"** (vs 1) - It is noteworthy that there are "doubtful things" for us to address in our lives. These are matters that do not have a heavenly clear directive.

- **"For one believes he may eat all things, but he who is weak eats only vegetables"** (vs 2) - Why is the one who eats only vegetables considered weak in faith? It is because they are trying to produce their own righteousness instead of believing what Jesus has done for them. We are considered weak if we believe that God is more interested in what we are doing than believing (see verse 17).

- **"Let not him who eats despise him who does not eat, and let not him who does not eat judge him who eats; for God has received him"** (vs 3) - We are to not despise (think badly about) those who are weak in faith (who believe true spirituality is measured by choosing not to do certain things).

- **"Who are you to judge another's servant? To his own master he stands or falls. Indeed, he will be made to stand, for God is able to make him stand"** (vs 4) - If we are focused on judging others, we are working against God's grace in those we judge. We are to believe they "will be made to stand" (they will be empowered by God to Christian maturity).

- **"One person esteems one day above another; another esteems every day alike. Let each be fully convinced in his own mind"** (vs 5) - We are to be fully convinced about what we do and what we believe. And it is possible concerning doubtful things that two people will have a different opinion and both be right.

- **"But why do you judge your brother? Or why do you show contempt for your brother? For we shall all stand before the judgment seat of Chris**t" (vs 10) - If we are regularly critiquing what others are doing and believing, then we are misguided. We are to take responsibility for our choices and beliefs because that is what we will give account for.

- **"Therefore let us not judge one another anymore, but rather resolve this, not to put a stumbling block or a cause to fall in our brother's way**" (vs 13) - We are to replace any tendency to judge others with the commitment to be a positive example to other believers, especially those who are weaker in the faith.

- **"I know and am convinced by the Lord Jesus that there is nothing unclean of itself; but to him who considers anything to be unclean, to him it is unclean**" (vs 14) - Our beliefs about whether our choices are right or wrong have a greater impact on our inner victory and influence than we might think.

- **"For the kingdom of God is not eating and drinking, but righteousness and peace and joy in the Holy Spiri**t" (vs 17) - If we pursue the depths of righteousness, peace, and joy, we will develop the beliefs and theology to experience the abundant life Jesus spoke about in John 10:10.

- **"It is good neither to eat meat nor drink wine nor do anything by which your brother stumbles or is offended or is made weak**" (vs 21) - As we remove the shackles of legalism and doubt, we should not allow this freedom to detach us from deep connections in the body of Christ (where we can make sure our freedom is rooted in love and positive influence). Certainly, not everyone is going to agree with our choices and beliefs, but we do need to be sensitive to the dynamics of the culture we are in and the people we are called to influence.

- **"Do you have faith? Have it to yourself before God. Happy is he who does not condemn himself in what he approves**" (vs 22) - We are to decide by connecting personally with the Lord what we "approve" of in many areas of life. We will be unhappy if we condemn ourselves for things we have previously approved. (Note: we may change our minds on what we approve of, but we need a good process of decision-making, and we must not be wishy-washy, regularly changing our minds).

- **"But he who doubts is condemned if he eats, because he does not eat from faith; for whatever is not from faith is sin**" (vs 23) - This chapter ends with the powerful statement that whatever we do apart from faith (attaching our faith) is sin. The original word in the Bible for the word sin is *hamartia*. The word hamartia means "missing the mark," derived from the sport of archery. As we attach faith to our beliefs and choices, we will "hit the mark" in our purpose, assignments, inner victory, and relationships. This verse is not to create a fear of punishment mindset of "If I don't have enough faith, I must be sinning", but it is to impress on us that what we believe is ultimately more important than what we do.

Romans 14 empowers us to develop our own convictions concerning "doubtful things" and then attach faith to what we decide. It is a chapter that brings much needed freedom into our lives. Yes, it is possible that some could use the chapter to justify doing things clearly opposed to God's will, but we cannot let this fear stop us from pursuing its truths. Remember, the same culture that created eleven world changers also created a Judas. Leaders who are focused on preventing a Judas will most liikely not have world changers. This is also true in how we lead ourselves. **If our primary goal in life is to try to prevent a Judas (poor behavior) from manifesting in us, we will almost assuredly not unlock the world changer that is inside us.** We may not know how to practically apply Romans 14, but as we trust God to give us wisdom, He will. Romans 14:4 gives us a promise that we will stand in fully convinced beliefs. "Indeed, (you) will be made to stand, for God is able to make (you) stand." It is exciting to see how God will do this.

With that said, let's summarize the fantastic truths from Romans 14 that will propel us to live a fully convinced lifestyle and to attach great faith to who we are and what we do:

- We are considered "weak in the faith" if we think what we do and don't do is the highest measurement of spirituality.
- We are to respect the choices of others concerning disputable matters. Two people can have different beliefs on what to do, or not do, and both be right.
- Being fully convinced in our own minds is an important aspect of Christian maturity.
- My belief that something is "unclean" (wrong) makes it unclean for me. Concerning these "doubtful things" our beliefs may change because of new assignments, new seasons, and different kinds of people we are to influence.
- Righteousness, peace, and joy are to be prioritized as we focus on what is important in the kingdom and pursue being fully convinced. Peace and joy might seem to be more positive focuses than righteousness, but that is not true. I suggest you go back to chapter two (The Power of Beliefs) and re-read the section entitled "Right Believing or Right Living?" This will give you a good understanding of why righteousness is one-third of the kingdom.

- We are to decide through our own relationship with God what we "approve" of in our behaviors and beliefs, and happiness is a main sign we have overcome condemning ourselves about what we have approved.
- Attaching faith to what we are doing causes us to "hit the mark" in our life's purpose, assignments, and relationships.

As we consider 2 Corinthians 9:7 and Romans 14, it becomes clear that attaching faith to what we do and who we are is a crucial part of our maturing as followers of Jesus. **I believe this being "fully convinced in our own minds" is a missing piece** for many who already value and are pursuing other aspects of Christ-likeness such as:

- Surrender
- Love
- Fruit of the Spirit
- Gifts of the Spirit
- Obedience
- Sacrificial living
- Humility
- Worship and intimacy with God
- Loving and honoring the Bible

By God's grace, we can expect these to become stronger in us. We are confident (fully convinced) that we are predestined to a process of being conformed to these attributes. The following verses tell us so: "For whom He foreknew, He also predestined to be conformed to the image of His Son" (Romans 8:29), and "Being confident of this very thing, that He who has begun a good work in you will complete it until the day of Jesus Christ" (Philippians 1:6). And again, we are also confident we will be conformed into a fully convinced/attaching faith lifestyle as this is promised to us in Hebrews 12:2, "Looking unto Jesus, the author and finisher of our faith."

Getting Practical

Here are some of the main concepts I shared in chapter two of this book that will help us move toward being fully convinced and attaching faith to who we are and what we do:

- There are four main mindsets we can have concerning our commitments and responsibilities: 1) Reluctance and compulsion, 2) Doubt, 3) Passivity, 4) Attaching faith

- When we attend to our commitments and responsibilities reluctantly or under compulsion (without faith), it is dead works. It is fascinating that the first two elementary principles of the kingdom speak to this; "Therefore, leaving the discussion of the elementary *principles* of Christ, let us go on to perfection, not laying again the foundation of repentance from dead works and of faith toward God" (Hebrews 6:1).

- A lack of cheerfulness is evidence we have not attached faith to what we are doing.

- When we attach faith to what we do and who we are, we will also get energy and power. Much of our tiredness is spiritual, not physical. When we are depressed, without hope, and without purpose, we will experience greater lethargy.

Before we go on, here are some questions and action steps to apply what we have been learning:

1. What main responsibilities and commitments are you doing reluctantly, under compulsion, passively, or in doubt? This could include areas like family, finances, work, ministry, spending time

with your children, resting, giving, going to church, or a biblical directive.

2. Which of these are the most important for you to address? For some, it will not be the biggest problem or biggest dream you want to address, but it will be something smaller so you can practice and gain momentum in attaching faith to your choices.

3. What areas of your life do you have guilt about? Which of these do you believe is a legitimate issue that needs you to do something now? (Many have low-grade guilt in life which robs them of life and energy. We will explore this more in the next chapter.)

4. Go through the process of decision-making described in chapter four to conclude what you are to believe and do about these things.

5. Speak declarations concerning your conclusions like the following:

   - I am called to be at this job, and I am significant.
   - I am to speak to that person about my concerns, and I will get a great plan from God for what to say and when to say it.
   - I am to live in this city, and my presence here is catalytic for God's purposes to be accomplished.
   - It is not my season to try to lose weight but I am to focus on _____.
   - I love sowing my taxes into my government.

Attaching Faith Through Declarations

"For with the heart one believes unto righteousness, and with the mouth confession is made unto salvation" (Romans 10:10).

We believe AND confess. Belief changes our identity (unto righteousness) and our confession is what changes our experience (salvation which literally means saved, healed, and delivered). They are both necessary, When we believe we are righteous, we will increasingly make righteous choices.

We use our words to give life to the "dead things" we are feeling and experiencing. "God, who gives life to the dead and calls those things which do not exist as though they did" (Romans 4:17). As we speak life, we will create life. Here are some examples:

- Today is a day of victory and breakthrough.
- My prayers for my family are working.
- God is meeting all my needs today.
- This is going to be a powerful and productive meeting.
- Many will get healed in tomorrow's church service.
- My marriage is experiencing breakthrough.

"Death and life are in the power of the tongue, and those who love it will eat its fruit" (proverbs 18:21). We will experience good fruit tomorrow by speaking life today.

"For we all stumble in many things. If anyone does not stumble in word, he *is* a perfect man, able also to bridle the whole body" (James 3:2). If we can control our words, we can control our lives.

"Indeed, we put bits in horses' mouths that they may obey us, and we turn their whole body. Look also at ships: although they are so large and are driven by fierce winds, they are turned by a very small rudder wherever the pilot desires. Even so the tongue . . ." (James 3:3-5). The tongue is the directing agent of our lives. Whatever we talk much about, we get pulled toward. Where do you want to be in five years? One of the main things to help you get there is to call that desire that does not currently exist as though it did. We won't have something just by saying something, but saying something is necessary to having something.

But I Don't Want to Get Disappointed Again

There is mental warfare when we start considering declaring things higher than what we are feeling and experiencing. It is what happened to Gideon in Judges 6 when the angel told him, "God is with you, mighty warrior" (Judges 6:12). He resisted the word and spouted off reasons why he could not get his hopes up for something better for himself and his nation. Like Gideon, our internal warfare usually centers around not wanting to be disappointed, so we lower our expectations to protect ourselves from it.

Our negative strongholds hate hope. When we ask the question, "What do I need to believe to have hope in my life, or in this area of my life?", we are setting ourselves up to get revelations of the truths that will demolish these strongholds (overcoming the self-limiting, hope-hindering beliefs creating these fortresses in our thinking).

Yes, there is a risk of being disappointed again when we think about getting our hopes up, but consider this, there are two ways we can live. We can live a hopeless life and never be disappointed, or we can live a hope-filled life with occasional disappointment. It is this second option that has life in it. It has been said that faith is spelled RISK. Those who succeed most also seem to fail most. Courage, by its very definition, implies there is risk involved in what we are being courageous about. And, in this chapter, as we are focusing on attaching faith to who we are and what we do, it takes courage to declare things higher than what we are feeling or experiencing.

Good Sports Teams Are Not Pessimistic Before a Game

Let me say again that when we attach faith to who we are and what we do, we will experience energy, cheerfulness, and power.

Here's how this practically works for me. Most mornings when I wake up, I say words like these, "This is going to be a great day. This is a day of victory and breakthrough. This will be my best day yet spiritually, emotionally, relationally, financially, and in seeing prayers answered." When I say this, it usually does not feel true in any way. Some would say that I should not say such words in the morning, but I should wait until the day is over and then use my words to describe what my day was like. This may sound logical, but it is not the thinking of world-changers. We are not called to primarily use our words to describe our lives but to change our lives.

"Steve, what if you say it is going to be the best day of your life, and then it is not the best day of your life, and it actually turns out to be a really bad day?" This is a great question. In answering this, let's consider what good athletes do in the locker room before an important game. They do not tolerate pessimism, passivity, and players saying things like this: "I really don't want to be here. I hope we don't lose too badly. Let's just try not to get hurt. I cannot wait for this game to be over so we can go have some fun." If they have a good coach, they have been prepared for the game by building strength and endurance, sharpening their skills, understanding their individual roles, and having a plan to address the strengths and weaknesses of their opponent. These are important ways to prepare, but there is one more needed ingredient for success. The players need to be passionate, inspired, and energized.

This vital component is created primarily through motivational words spoken by the coaches and players.

We not only need a good plan and a strong skill set, but we also need a fire burning on the inside of us to do great things and make a difference. This is what I try to do in the morning. As I wake up, I imagine myself in a locker room before a game or match. I speak words of victory over myself and my day. When I speak these things, I usually don't feel what I am saying, but the moment I start attaching faith to the day through my declarations, I start feeling cheerful and energized (even if it is a very small change at first). I am my own coach, and I am learning to inspire myself.

"But Steve, you have not answered the question yet. What if you say it is going to be a great day and it is not? Aren't you just lying?" Well, what do athletes do when they speak victory and success before a game but still lose? Do they say, "That did not work. Let's be more pessimistic before the next game." No, they realize that to experience increased victory, they will go through a process that includes defeating negative mindsets about themselves and about their team. They are on a journey of transforming a losing culture into a winning culture. When I speak victory but experience defeat, I realize it is a process for me as well. I will keep getting better in how I do things, how I connect with people, and how I understand my opponent, and as I get better, I am going to prioritize growing in being enthusiastic and victorious internally. Truly, the pathway to success is to become successful on the inside when I don't look successful on the outside. Losing is not a failure, but it is an opportunity to learn and grow stronger in my mind.

Seeding the Clouds of Our Future

Just like an athlete, we can inspire ourselves through declaring victory and excellence, but we can also create a better future with our faith-filled words - seeding the clouds of our future. Cloud seeding is a type of weather modification that aims to change the amount or type of precipitation that falls from clouds. I like to imagine a cloud over future events and future seasons in my life. Unfortunately, in the past, I would seed these clouds with negative thinking and negative words. Then when I began learning about how my negativity was self-sabotaging my future, I began to realize I needed to seed my future positively through my thoughts and words. Declarations are a great way to do this.

The Declaration Clicker

I have a goal to make at least 700 declarations a week (averaging 100+ a day). To help me do this, I have what I call a declaration clicker by my coffee pot in the morning. It helps me remember my locker room analogy, and I start right then, early in the morning, speaking faith-filled words to myself out loud. The clicker is a tally counter that you click for every declaration made. So I wake up in the morning and make my beginning declarations and then carry the declaration clicker with me throughout the day. It helps me attach faith to who I am and what I am doing.

Some of the most important declarations we make are concerning our commitments, assignments, and upcoming events and activities on our calendars. Here are examples of declarations that attach faith to these:

1. Tomorrow is going to be an incredible day.
2. This year is going to be the best year of my life spiritually, emotionally, relationally, financially, and in my influence.
3. My time with my family this weekend will cause a long-lasting blessing for generations to come.
4. The promises of God will manifest exponentially next month.
5. My sleep tonight will have supernatural dreams and wonderful rest.

6. The church service I will attend today will be our best one yet.
7. My 10 AM meeting with _____ will radically impact both our lives and have a 300 year impact on this city.
8. My relationship with my spouse this week will be absurdly good.
9. This week is a week of breakthrough in my emotions, relationships, finances, and Influence.
10. This will be the best week for me at work ever.
11. The conversations I have this month with my family will have an implausible positive influence on our relationships.
12. Every attack and every demonic assignment this month will not have any effect on me.
13. Tomorrow, my Kingdom influence will be greater than it has ever been.
14. This prayer time with the Lord will be astonishing.
15. When I walk into this room, everything changes. Every hopeless situation ceases to exist.

When we attach faith to what we are doing with declarations like this, we will find something wonderful happening in and through us. This is a major part of applying what I believe the Lord told me years ago, "Steve, instead of waiting to do something great, why don't you attach great faith to what you are doing now and it will become great?" We don't have to wait for IT to happen, we can make IT happen. Now let's go do it. Eternity will be glad we did.

Conclusion

"He who would love life and see good days, let him refrain his tongue from evil, and his lips from speaking deceit" (1 Peter 3:10). The habit of attaching faith to who we are and what we do will empower us greatly in loving life and seeing good days. Let's attach faith to the reading of this chapter right now and say: The contents of this chapter will increasingly bear massive fruit in me and those I influence.

CHAPTER 6

Empowered Toward Great Decisions (Increasing the Likelihood of Powerful Choices)

We weren't planning on buying a piano that day!

When we were newly married, Wendy and I decided to go to Eureka, CA, on a day off. It was the "big city" near us, and we thought it would be fun to walk around town enjoying each other and the city. While doing so, we walked by a piano store, and drawn by what we saw through the window, we decided to "go in and look around". Wendy wanted to learn to play the piano, but we did not have near enough finances to pay for one. Well, after about an hour in the store, a very persuasive salesman talked us into a five-year loan for a piano that we had no intention of buying and that unnecessarily stretched our budget.

Ugh. That is not the only decision we felt compelled to make that did not turn out well. However, on the other side of the coin, we have also made great decisions that seemed beyond our ability to make. One of these was inviting a man named Bill Johnson to be our guest speaker at the small church we were pastoring in Nevada in 1991. When we invited Bill, I had been feeding on people with big faith and possibility thinking, and I took the risk (financially and in other ways) to have him come and speak to our congregation. It was one of the best things I have ever done because it accelerated my personal growth and my leadership skills exponentially. As I look back on this decision, I recognize God's grace empowered me to make this choice.

In this chapter, we will focus on the factors that create good or bad decision-making tendencies. If we have the fruit of good decisions, then there are reasons for this, and if we are prone to make poor choices, then there are reasons for this as well. Whichever way, there are root causes to our choices. As we understand these roots, and then replace negative roots with positive ones, we will be propelled to catalytic decision-making by a spiritual force called grace.

Grace is the empowerment to do God's will. It is a spiritual force that creates obedience and Christlikeness. It is an inward compulsion resulting from a spiritual heart change. "This is the covenant that I will make with them after those days, says the Lord: I will put My laws into their hearts, and in their minds, I will write them," *then He adds,* 'Their sins and their lawless deeds I will remember no more'" (Hebrews 10:16-17).

There are beliefs and priorities that will help us increase this grace flowing into our lives. We have already discussed many of these, but I want to go deeper.

Factors Creating Good Decisions

Here are thirteen factors that will dramatically increase the likelihood of us making good decisions.

1. **Consuming, Meditating On, and Speaking God's Word** - In Joshua 1:8, Joshua, a new leader, is on the edge of the promised

land. He is told to be courageous and very strong. God also says to him, "This book of the law shall not depart from your mouth, but you shall meditate on it day and night that you may observe to do all that is written therein. Then you will make your way prosperous and be of good success" (Joshua 1:8). This verse is one of the most powerful verses in the Bible to be propelled into good decisions. It says if we don't let God's truths depart from our mouths, and if we meditate on His words, then **it will cause us** to do what's written in it. Another verse in the Bible says, "I have hid Your word in my heart, that I might not sin against you" (Psalm 119:11). Finally, Jesus reinforced this in John 8:31-32, "So Jesus said to the Jews who had believed him, 'If you abide in My word, you are truly my disciples, and you will know the truth, and the truth will set you free." The power of God's word is incredible. The more we get it on the inside of us, the more we will make great decisions.

2. **Being Filled With the Holy Spirit** - Something incredible happens when we are filled/baptized with the Holy Spirit. It is supernatural empowerment toward boldness, miracles, and setting others free. The last command Jesus gave to his disciples is in Acts 1: "And being assembled together with them, He commanded them not to depart from Jerusalem, but to wait for the Promise of the Father, 'which', He said, 'you have heard from Me; for John truly baptized with water, but you shall be baptized with the Holy Spirit not many days from now.'" Jesus goes on to say, "But you shall receive power when the Holy Spirit has come upon you; and you shall be witnesses to Me in Jerusalem, and in all Judea and Samaria, and to the end of the earth" (Acts 1:4-8). This was fulfilled on the Day of Pentecost which propelled struggling believers to overcome self-preservation thinking and step into a life of heroic decision-making marked by love, sacrifice, courage, and heavenly values. Their experience of

being filled with the Holy Spirit was not a one-time event. "And when they had prayed, the place where they were assembled together was shaken; and they were all filled with the Holy Spirit, and they spoke the word of God with boldness" (Acts 4:31). This Holy Spirit power is still available for us today. As we hunger for and believe in the fullness of the Spirit in our lives, we will experience one of the most important sources of great decision-making (supernatural power).

3. **Receiving the Abundance of Grace and the Gift of Righteousness According to Romans 5:17** - Understanding grace and the finished work of the cross will positively impact our decisions. If we have an Old Testament "works of the law" mentality (trying to perform for love, acceptance, and blessings), rather than a "beliefs and looking to Jesus" mentality, we will actually increase sin (poor choices). According to Romans 5:20, "Now the law came in to increase the trespass." The law reveals our sinful nature and the need for a divine solution for us to choose rightly. The more we focus on trying not to sin, the more we will sin; but the more we "consider ourselves dead to sin and alive to God in Christ Jesus" (Romans 6:11), the stronger our choices will be. We will be "alive to God " in what we choose to the proportion we receive "grace" and the "gift of righteousness" (right standing with God). "For if, because of one man's trespass, death reigned through that one man, much more will those who receive the abundance of grace and the free gift of righteousness reign in life through the one man Jesus Christ" (Romans 5:20).

4. **Walking with the Wise** - "He started hanging out with the wrong crowd." We have all probably heard this said about someone who spiraled into horrible decisions. Proverbs 13:20 says, "He who walks with the wise will be wise." Who we spend time with and who we allow to influence us will largely indicate

what our own decisions will be. Wise people are people who make good decisions. So, if we want to be an eagle (making eagle decisions), we must find a way to hang out with eagles. Even if we cannot be with them in person, we can be with them in books, in church, through podcasts, online things, etc. and that will greatly increase our decision-making ability.

5. **Controlling Our Speech** - "And if anyone does not stumble in what he says, he is a perfect man, able also to bridle his whole body" (James 3:2). If we can control what we say, we can control our whole life. Ephesians 4:29 says, "Let no corrupt word proceed out of your mouth, but what is good for necessary edification, that it may impart grace to the hearers." Impartation is a supernatural release of grace into our lives. Again, grace is the empowerment to do (obey) what God wants us to do. Let me say it again: grace empowers us towards obedience. We can receive grace through what we say and hear, "...but what is good for necessary edification, that it may impart grace to the hearers." As I declare God's promises and my biblical identity, I impart grace to myself to make higher choices in life.

6. **Fellowship with Other Believers** - "But if we walk in the light as He is in the light, we have fellowship with one another, and the blood of Jesus Christ His Son cleanses us from all sin" (1 John 1:7). The word "fellowship" comes from the Greek word "koinonia". This is an intimate spiritual communion in a Christ-honoring community. It is much more than just attending church, it is highly relational and interactive. 1 John 1:7 tells us that this kind of relationship has the power to cleanse us from all sin (from missing the mark for our lives). A lifestyle of "koinonia" empowers us toward good choices.

7. **Humility** - "But He gives more grace. Therefore He says: 'God resists the proud, but gives grace to the humble'" (James 4:6). God empowers (gives grace to) the humble. Humility is a quality where: 1) we are aware of our own short-comings (which causes us to not be judgmental or condescending toward others), 2) we believe we can learn something from every person, and 3) we recognize who we are is primarily the result of the investment of God and people. Humility causes us to believe we cannot live successfully without the help of God and other people. It is my observation we all have at least one area in our lives where we need help from someone else to make sure we don't do something stupid or just slowly move into a life of mediocrity or compromise. This weakness is actually a blessing and an invitation to humble ourselves to a counselor, trusted friend, leader, or someone else. As we do, we will find empowering grace flowing into our lives.

8. **Delighting in the Lord** - "Delight yourself in the Lord, and He will give you the desires of your heart" (Psalm 37:4). Delighting in the Lord is a child-like wonder and excitement about who God is, who we are in Him, and what He is going to do. As we delight while waiting for desires to be fulfilled, we will help cause what we desire to come into our experience. One desire we all have is to make better decisions. **Delighters are better decision-makers because they magnify the Lord, not their own abilities.** Delighting in the Lord is a key to having a prosperous soul. "Beloved, I pray that you may prosper in all things and be in health, just as your soul prospers" (3 John 2). Those who "prosper in all things" do so because their souls are prospering through good beliefs fueling good choices.

9. **Vision for the Future** - Proverbs 29:18 says "without a prophetic vision, the people cast off restraint." A vision is a purpose, goal,

or dream that motivates us to sacrifice to accomplish it. Vision for the future gives purpose and power to the present. The more vision that I have that my life is significant, that my future will be better than the present, that I have the power to make things better, and that I am going to be doing greater things in the days ahead, then the more I will be propelled to make more powerful decisions now. I will find myself asking the question, "Will this choice cause me to get closer to accomplishing my vision?" And the stronger this vision is, the stronger my motivation will be to be intentional in my decision-making. I will choose to not do certain things that may hinder that vision but instead, I will opt to do the things that will lead toward that vision becoming reality. "Where there is no prophetic vision, the people cast off restraint." Without a prophetic vision, our lives become undisciplined in how we think and what we do.

10. **Moving Forward in Life** - This is similar in some ways to having a vision. In Exodus 14:15, God said to Moses, "Why do you cry to Me? Tell the children of Israel to go forward." Moving forward seemed ridiculous because the Red Sea was before them and the Egyptians were closing in on them from behind. Even so, once they started moving forward the Red Sea parted and the Egyptians were defeated. Say this declaration: **My forward movement causes Red Seas to part**. One of the most important questions we can ask is, "How can I move forward today and in this season?" It may be as simple as cleaning out your car, or it could be a bigger choice like attending a particular school. People who are moving forward in life, and moving towards something, are going to gain **momentum** which will positively influence the choices they make. On the other hand, if we are passive, or just reacting to what is happening in life, then our choices will tend to focus on self-preservation rather than on taking us somewhere better.

11. **Becoming Responsible for Others** - When we assume responsibility for others, we experience good pressure to be a role model and an example in how we live. The Apostle Peter says this to church elders, "(Not) being lords over those entrusted to you, but being examples to the flock" (1 Peter 5:3). It is natural when somebody has children or assumes a leadership role that they upgrade their choices to set a good example for those they are influencing. However, isolated, non-contributing people will be much more likely to make poor choices because they do not have the natural accountability that responsibility brings.

12. **Embracing Seeming Failure as We Go Higher** - Those who succeed most also seem to fail most. Winston Churchill said, "Success is moving from failure to failure without losing enthusiasm." When toddlers learn to walk, they go through an apparent season of failure before walking well. Just because we struggle to "walk well" in an area of life (public speaking, leadership, emotional success, school, etc.), does not automatically mean we are not gifted and called into that area. High-level decision-makers are people who do not let failure define them. They realize the only way they can fail at something is by not doing anything at all. "For a righteous man may fall seven times and rise again" (Proverbs 24:16).

13. **Rest and Have Balance in Our Lives** - The great Prophet Elijah made poor decisions and poor conclusions because of tiredness, hunger, and fear (see 1 Kings 19). He had just participated in one of history's greatest events when he called down fire from heaven to consume a soaking wet sacrifice and thus proved Jehovah is the one true God. Even so, Elijah was ready to choose suicide because of his poor physical and emotional state. Part of the remedy to overcome this depression was to sleep and eat. Once he did this and connected with the heart of God, he

rebounded and then anointed three men for key assignments for the future. We too would be wise to get enough sleep, eat well, exercise, and have hobbies to help keep us physically and emotionally healthy. As we do, we will find greater strength and energy to make better decisions than if we did not take care of ourselves.

Root Causes Creating Bad Decisions

We have looked at thirteen factors creating good decisions. Now let's address root causes that negatively impact our choices. Unless these roots are addressed, we will be prone to make poor choices no matter how much we want to make good ones. Here is a list of some factors that may be affecting our ability to make great decisions. You will notice some similarities with our list of positive influences but the repetition will reinforce important truths for you.

1. **Bad Company or Negative Relationships in Our Lives** - Again, the people we "hang out" with, or that we spend time with (whether in person or through media), will have a huge effect on our behavior. "Do not be deceived: 'Evil company corrupts good habits'" (1 Corinthians 15:33).

2. **Poor Identity Beliefs** - In Numbers 13, the ten spies said, "We were like grasshoppers in our own sight, and so we were in their sight" (vs 33). They made a poor decision to not pursue their promises (to not pursue their potential) because of who they thought they were. If we believe we are a low-level person, we will make low-level decisions.

3. **Renewing the Mind with Lies** - Romans 12:2 says, "Be transformed by the renewing of your mind." This is obviously talking about positively renewing our minds with truth, but

we can renew our minds with lies as well (based on negative feelings and negative past experiences). Here is a powerful truth: whatever we renew our minds with, we transform our future to. Current mind renewal creates future experiences. If we are mainly rehearsing lies in our thinking about our identity, our potential, and the circumstances we face, we will be unable to make quality decisions.

4. **Works of the Law Focused** - Being law-focused actually creates sin in our lives. "The law entered that the offense might abound" (Romans 5:20). As stated before, sin means "to miss the mark". Sin is making bad decisions or lower decisions than we are designed to make. If we're under an Old Testament mindset of focusing on obedience to God's laws (rather than prioritizing our beliefs and relationship with Him), then that focus will cause us to make wrong choices. Please note: If we are struggling with unrighteous behaviors, I am not saying we should not get help from skilled and anointed people, but our greatest emphasis cannot be on giving ourselves rules to obey.

5. **Negative Speech** - We will not be a positive decision-maker if we are a person of negative speech. We cannot speak defeat and have victory. "Death and life are in the power of the tongue, and those who love it will eat its fruit" (Proverbs 18:21). Those who love what? Those who love the revelation that life is in the power of the tongue will eat the positive fruit of their life-filled words. But there is also the truth that death is in the power of the tongue. If we are regularly speaking negatively, that will actually work against our ability to make good choices. James 3 says our words are like a bit in a horse's mouth or a rudder on a ship (vs 3 and 4). Our words direct the course of our lives. So whatever we talk a lot about, we will get pulled towards. If we regularly say, "We can't do that", then we will come to a place

where we will be making decisions based on that assertion, and we will choose to not do what we actually can do. And if we have the habit of saying, "I am so tired," we will experience more tiredness and this will hinder us from making good choices.

6. **Perfectionism** - A perfectionist is someone who strives to be flawless and to experience no mistakes around them. They fixate on imperfections, trying to control situations, working hard, and/or being critical of themselves or others. Perfectionism and the religious mindset are very similar. They are at the root of the thinking of the one who buried his talent in Matthew 25. He decided to do this because of a fear of not doing things perfectly and a fear of punishment from his master. Those who are unwilling to go through a process that involves some form of struggle and apparent failure (while growing in their gifts and talents) will make poor decisions by not attempting to do what they are capable of doing.

7. **Being Disconnected From Christ** - When we're not yielded to God and the Holy Spirit, and we're doing our own thing, we are blocked from the flow of the Spirit in our lives. This will result in us producing the works of the flesh mentioned in Galatians 5:19-21. These works include a whole host of bad decisions including adultery, fornication, idolatry, envy, and angry outbursts. Jesus said, "I am the vine, you are the branches. He who abides in Me, and I in him, bears much fruit; for without Me you can do nothing" (John 15:5).

8. **Generational Curses and Past Trauma** - A generational curse is a negative behavioral tendency passed down through family generations creating bad beliefs and ultimately bad decisions. Even though when we are born again, we become a new creation and become spiritually free from such curses (John 3:3;

2 Corinthians 5:17), there is still sometimes a need to directly deal with negative traits passed down to us by renouncing them, forgiving our parents and ancestors, and receiving anointed and wise ministry from people concerning these tendencies. This not only applies to generational curses but may also be necessary for trauma we have experienced in the past.

These root causes are contributors to bad choices. As we address them and other negative factors that influence our decision-making, we will find ourselves in a place where it's much easier to not miss the mark in our lives and callings. However, let me say this again, even though we need to be aware of the root causes of poor choices, we cannot primarily be thinking about preventing wrong-doing in our lives.

Great Decision-Makers Are Not Mainly Focused on Preventing Wrong Choices

Are good decision-makers only those who do not do bad things? The Old Testament law emphasized what not to do: not lying, not stealing, not committing adultery, etc. It was a "prevent wrong from happening" priority. There is certainly value in pursuing good character and integrity, but that is not the highest level of what a great decision-maker is. As I consider this, I am drawn to Romans 5:3-4 where it says, "But we glory in tribulation, knowing that tribulation worketh perseverance, perseverance character, and character hope". It's a great four-step message on how to win in life that goes beyond seeing "good character" as our goal.

Firstly, when we are experiencing life challenges, we are to "glory" in God. We find Him in the middle of the tribulation. We rejoice, speak His promises, and stir up thanksgiving. Secondly, we persevere in this "glorying". We keep at it and don't quit. As we keep persevering, we move to the third step and develop what's called character, which is living by godly core values. Our lives are no longer driven by emotion in decision-making, but by core values and God's spiritual laws. We become convinced about not sacrificing our future for temporary pleasure.

I used to think having character was the highest level of living, and, yes, it is an important level of living, but there's something even greater than that. It's called hope. This higher level is not focused on behavior but on beliefs. As I've said before, hope is the belief that the future will be better than the present, and we have the power to help make it so. Hope results from having good beliefs.

The kingdom of God is not primarily moved forward by good behavior, but it is moved forward by good beliefs. I have said this before - what we believe is ultimately more important than what we do. The question of the hour is not, "Lord, what should I do?" The greater question is, "Lord, what should I believe? What beliefs do you want me to renew my mind with in the days ahead?" A perspective of hope is a big indicator we are renewing our minds with truth and not lies (Romans 15:13). Hope is a catalytic attitude in life. Our hope level determines our influence level, and he who has the most hope has the most influence.

So, what is the focus of a great decision-maker? A great decision-maker is not obsessed with repressing negative behaviors (sin). Again, sin means to miss the mark. Missing the mark is missing that which we were designed to do - missing our highest calling and our highest potential in life. The one-talent person in Matthew 25 missed the mark in his life. His decision to bury his talent was based on trying to prevent negative things from happening by focusing on not doing something wrong. His mindset and choices were certainly not celebrated by Jesus in the parable. The other two servants (the one who received five talents and the one who received two) had abundance mindsets, made great decisions, and increased their talents. They provide a great illustration of those who are not mainly focused on preventing wrong choices in their lives. And, do you know what really encourages me about the Parable of the Talents? It is this: two out of three had a perspective of hope and made forward-moving decisions. That tells me there will be more of us who make great decisions than those who don't.

As we consider this and believe for it, we will find ourselves being propelled by God to go beyond just preventing negative behaviors and choices. We will actually move into a greater perspective of hope which will cause us to make decisions that unlock the greatness in us and others. We will increasingly believe we have a great future and that we will make a significant difference in the world. This perspective will show us how big our potential is, enable us to activate the gifts within, and give us the courage to not be afraid of apparent failure in our journey to increase our talents and become what we never thought we could become.

When we truly understand that making choices driven by preventing wrongdoing severely cripples our decision-making, and then choose to live with an awareness of the grace and hope available to us, even in instances where we seem to be "failing", we will be able to attach faith to whatever we choose to do and avoid the trap of guilt motivated decisions.

Overcoming Guilt Motivated Decision-Making

Let's again examine the phrase, "A bad decision made in faith has a greater likelihood of success than a good decision made in doubt." In non-black and white areas of life, God says, "Clarify your options, receive my wisdom, decide what to believe and do, and then attach faith (become fully convinced) about that." It is the practical outworking of Romans 14:5: "One person esteems one day above another; another esteems every day alike. Let each be fully convinced in his own mind."

In this verse, we are told, "Let each be fully convinced in his own mind" concerning what to believe about Sabbaths. Being "fully convinced" is the goal of our decision-making. I know from personal experience that I was rarely able to attach faith to what I was doing or believing because of a haunting feeling I could be wrong. For instance, if I was made aware of a need, but decided not to meet that need, I would frequently feel guilty about my decision afterward. I was not fully convinced about what I was choosing to do or not to do. Also, there were many times I would choose to help meet the need, but it was from a place of feeling obligated to do so. In this too, my decision wasn't made in faith.

These tendencies are not ones we can take with us if we want to go to the next level of decision-making. 2 Corinthians 9:7 says we are to give cheerfully, not reluctantly or under compulsion, but it is also true that if we choose not to give, we are to do that cheerfully as well. I believe God will train all of us to give in faith and also not give in faith. He will train us to go to the meeting in faith and not go to the meeting in faith. If we have the habit of making impulsive decisions about doing something or not doing something, we will often live in regret and doubt about what we are doing. We are to be like Peter in Acts 11 when he was led by the Holy Spirit to fellowship with the Gentiles, and he was to move forward in this "doubting nothing" (Acts 11:12).

So what do you feel guilty about that you're either doing or not doing? You might want to go back to chapter one and re-read the "Never Enough Lie" or "Defeating Unsuspecting Sources of Shame" to help you determine this. One area I have struggled with concerns how much to give to specific relationships in my life. I have felt guilty for not connecting more with some people, while in other situations I have felt forced into giving time and emotional energy to certain people. God has told me, "Just decide what you are going to do or not do, and then attach faith to it." I am sure you can relate to this. Whether it is relational or something else, it is important to go after the root reasons for the

EMPOWERED TOWARD GREAT DECISIONS

guilt we feel. We do this by clarifying our options, going through the decision-making process again, and then deciding what to do or not do. Once you have done this, attack any feelings of guilt and develop the "doubting nothing" muscle. What I am sharing with you here is a tremendous key to personal victory. Remember, a bad decision made in faith has a greater likelihood of success than a good decision made in doubt. There is power in attacking low-grade guilt in our lives. As we do, we will experience grace to make higher decisions.

Increasing the Likelihood of Making Great Decisions

This chapter is all about how not to feel compelled to buy an unnecessary piano, and how to be surprisingly empowered to make decisions like inviting Bill Johnson to be your guest speaker. As you have thought through its content, what is standing out to you? What one or two significant adjustments do you need to make to increase the likelihood of making great decisions?

I love the concept of "increasing the likelihood of good things happening." Let me illustrate with some examples:

- Attending church services increases the likelihood of victory and breakthrough for me.
- Declaring "this is going to be a great day" increases the likelihood that it will be a great day for me.
- Reading a book on finances increases the likelihood of financial success in my life.
- Signing up for gym membership with a friend increases the likelihood of me getting more physically fit.
- Increasing my thanksgiving to God and people increases the likelihood of emotional health in my life.

- Regularly speaking encouraging words to my children increases the likelihood of their success and my having a good relationship with them.

Conclusion

You might say, "Steve, this is good teaching, but I have already made bad decisions in my life. I wish I would have followed this wisdom, but I did not. I really regret my choices and am now living with negative consequences as a result. What should I do?"

Here's my advice. Strengthen your decision-making skills now and then decide what you are going to do and believe about your regrets. Clarify your options, go through the process of concluding, and then attach faith to what you decide. For instance, you will have options for what actions to take (apologize to someone, make restitution, or do nothing but stand in faith that God is turning the situation to good, etc.), and you will have options for what to believe (I am shameful, I am less than, I am forgiven, God is turning this to good, etc.). What we decide about areas of regret are some of the most important decisions we make in our lives.

"Father, thank You that You are empowering us toward great decisions. Thank You that You will complete the good work you started in us."

CHAPTER 7

Limitless Living

"Buddy, when are you going to eat your food?"

I mentioned my dog, Buddy, in chapter one when I highlighted the words, "Buddy, will you just decide whether you want to come in or if you want to stay outside?!" (By the way, the Lord keeps saying to me in key areas of my life, "Steve will you just decide! Will you decide what you are going to do and what you are going to believe, and will you attach faith to that so you can hit the mark in what I have purposed for you.")

When we got Buddy, we also had another dog named Duncan, who was a black lab and was in his final year of life then. It was interesting to note the differences between Buddy and Duncan when they were given food to eat. Duncan, who had a poverty mindset, would quickly consume his food and eat every last bit. Buddy, who had an abundance mindset, would be in no hurry to eat his food but would wait until a later time to eat because he seemed to believe there was an abundance of food for him that would keep on coming. This is a chapter to inspire us to be like Buddy and believe there is always more available to us.

As I share this, I am reminded of my grandson Caden. When he was about three, I asked him this question, "Caden, how come you have so many good ideas?" He said, "Well, when I run out of good ideas, God gives me more." I thought, "When I grow up, I want to be like Caden. He thinks there is a non-ending flow of ideas coming to him that will cause him to continually make great decisions in his life. I want to think like that."

I have battled survivalistic and fatalistic thinking like most of you. I have had times of being plagued by the "Duncan syndrome" of focusing primarily on getting my needs met in the moment rather than pursuing big dreams for my future. Certainly, there are seasons and situations where this is necessary, but many, like Duncan, stay in that mindset when it is totally unnecessary. God has put a desire to experience big and great things in our lives inside each of us.

As I think of this, I am struck by this thought: If God wanted us to think small and with limitations, he sure did a bad job in telling us so. Consider these verses:

- John 10:10 - "The thief does not come except to steal, and to kill, and to destroy. I have come that they may have life, and that they may have it more abundantly."
- Mark 9:23 - "All things are possible to him who believes."
- Luke 1:37 - "For with God nothing will be impossible."
- Ephesians 3:20 - "Now to Him who is able to do exceedingly abundantly above all that we ask or think, according to the power that works in us."
- Mark 11:24 - "Therefore I say to you, whatever things you ask when you pray, believe that you receive them, and you will have them."
- Philippians 4:13 - "I can do all things through Christ who strengthens me.

- Psalm 91:17 - "A thousand may fall at your side, and ten thousand at your right hand; but it shall not come near you."
- Psalm 1:2-3 - "And in His law he meditates day and night . . . and whatever he does shall prosper."
- John 14:12 - "Most assuredly, I say to you, he who believes in Me, the works that I do he will do also; and greater works than these he will do, because I go to My Father."
- Matthew 14:29 - "Peter walked on the water to go to Jesus."
- Romans 6:11 - "Likewise you also, reckon yourselves to be dead indeed to sin, but alive to God in Christ Jesus our Lord."
- 2 Corinthians 5:17 - "Therefore, if anyone is in Christ, he is a new creation; old things have passed away; behold, all things have become new."
- Galatians 2:20 - "I have been crucified with Christ; it is no longer I who live, but Christ lives in me."
- Galatians 3:13 - "Christ has redeemed us from the curse of the law, having become a curse for us."

These and many other Bible verses invite us to think big and dream big about what is possible in life. They are an invitation for us to decide to become spiritual explorers and spiritual experimenters to find the unchartered territories of the abundant life that Jesus promised us in John 10:10. Just as Christopher Columbus set sail to find lands that the experts of the day were not even sure existed, we too can "set sail" for a type of living that no one has experienced before. "But as it is written: 'Eye has not seen, nor ear heard, nor have entered into the heart of man the things which God has prepared for those who love Him.' But God has revealed them to us through His Spirit" (1 Corinthians 2:9-10)

Our belief that there is more to be experienced causes hunger in our hearts and creates a massive upgrade in our decision-making. It causes us:

- To be dissatisfied with the status-quo
- To take greater risks
- To be future-focused instead of past-focused

"Brethren, I do not count myself to have apprehended; but one thing I do, forgetting those things which are behind and **reaching forward to those things which are ahead**" (Philippians 3:13). There is no limit to the amount of "those things" we can reach forward to. As we become increasingly fully convinced about this, we will move past survivalism and into incredible possibilities for our lives. Let's delve deeper into limitless living and limitless thinking.

Building on a Solid Foundation

We have emphasized much about attaching great faith to what we are doing now and then seeing it become great. Once we have this revelation of the importance of attaching faith to who we are and what we do, we have the proper foundation for radically increasing our talents (Matthew 25:14-30), bearing 100-fold fruit (Matthew 13:23), dreaming big dreams for our lives (Genesis 37:1-11), and for living a lifestyle that far exceeds what we thought was possible (Ephesians 3:20). The "attaching great faith" mindset is a strong antidote to the pesky "I am a victim" mentality, which wants to continually tell us, "You are at a disadvantage and cannot expect amazing things for your life and influence."

Oh, that pesky victim mindset. I used to think I was a victim of four things; 1) My past, 2) the people in my life, 3) the devil, and 4) a preordained plan of God that put limits on me. It's this last mindset that is very subtle and damaging to our potential. I did not verbalize this belief, but I subconsciously had it as a result of what I heard other Christians say. I thought God had predestined some to be level ten Christians, while I believed I was predestined to be a level three. And if I really sacrificed, I might be able to get up to 3.1. (Haha). I now know this is a lie.

This chapter, "Limitless Living", is designed to help us defeat self-limiting mindsets and move us into a lifestyle of no limits. Romans 12:2 is an important verse for us to do so. It has many great truths in it, but let's focus on two of them now.

1. **Current Mind Renewal Creates Future Experience** - Whatever I renew my mind with today will transform my experience in the future. For instance, if I renew my mind that I powerfully influence nations, then I will transform my future into powerfully influencing nations. It will work for everybody. However, if I renew my mind with the lie that I am a person who is inferior to others and has little favor, then I will transform my future into feelings of inferiority and an experience of having little favor.

2. **Because There is no Limit to How Much I Can Renew My Mind, Then There is no Limit to How Much I Can Be Transformed** - Nobody's past can stop their future but current beliefs can. Let me say that again: Nobody's past can stop their future but current beliefs can. The past by itself does not have the power to limit our tomorrow, but the conclusions we make based on our past can. We cannot change our past, but we can change how we think now. This is exciting because the only thing that we really can become a victim of is our own thinking. This gives us great hope because, again, there is no limit to how much we can renew our minds, so there is no limit to how much we can be transformed.

Let me illustrate how certain people's beliefs limited the experience they could have had. In Mark 6:1-6, Jesus visited his hometown. We are told He could only do a few miracles there because of the beliefs that the people had about him. Because they saw Him only as "Joseph's son", they did not experience God's plan for their lives or region. It was God's predestined plan that Jesus' hometown be a place of great miracles, but their beliefs restricted what they could have experienced. **This story is important to meditate on because many believers subconsciously believe that what they are experiencing (and the level of freedom and breakthrough they have) is a predetermined plan of God for them** (based on His will or based on their own worthiness)**. These faulty conclusions create passivity, fatalism, and an inability to contend for promises to manifest.** As we increasingly understand the need to address our self-limiting beliefs, we will start to unlock the potential that is in us like never before.

The Flea and the Elephant

To help us understand the destructive power of self-limiting beliefs, let's consider fleas and elephants.

The Flea – If you put fleas in a jar and place a lid on the jar, the fleas will learn to jump just high enough to avoid hitting the lid. Then when the lid is removed, the fleas will not jump out (even with the lid gone).

The Baby Elephant – In India, elephant trainers place a chain around a baby elephant's leg attached to a three-foot iron stake which is driven into the ground. For several days, the baby elephant tries to free itself from the stake and chain but cannot. Soon, it is convinced by this experience that the three-foot stake and chain determine how much freedom it has. It no longer attempts to pull free. Ten years later, when the elephant is fully grown (weighing thousands of pounds and capable of uprooting trees or pulling a loaded railway car) it can still be held by a three-foot stake!

These are fascinating examples to ponder. Many of our "logical" beliefs are actually just the result of renewing our minds with our experiences rather than with truth.

How can we get past the supposed lids and chains in our lives?

1. **Realize They Have Either Already Been Removed or Have the Power to Restrain Us** – "If anyone is in Christ, he is a new creation; old things have passed away; behold, all things have become new" (2 Corinthians 5:17). They can no longer hold us in our new identity in Christ.

2. **Don't Get Your Beliefs From Your Feelings or From the Past** – We don't deny our feelings or the past, we just cannot get our beliefs from them. In 2 Corinthians 10:4-5, we are called to pull down strongholds and demolish arguments that are exalting themselves above the knowledge of God. The two greatest arguments trying to exalt themselves above the knowledge of God are feelings and past experience.

3. **Step Out of the Boat** – Peter took a risk and walked on water (Matthew 14:22-33). He found "the walking on water lid" was off by taking a risk and stepping out of the boat. He was not 100% successful, but he tried. Some have criticized the church I am a part of because we recently had an extended time of praying for the resurrection of a baby who died, but I am very proud of our church for doing this. Often, new levels of breakthrough are on the other side of new levels of risk.

4. **Stop Speaking Self-Limiting Words** – When God called Jeremiah to be a prophet, he said, "'Ah, Lord God! Behold, I do not know how to speak, for I am only a youth.' But the Lord said to me, 'Do not say, "I am only a youth"'" (Jeremiah 1:6-7).

Many reinforce imaginary lids because of false humility and undisciplined speech.

5. **Memorize and Meditate on the Verses at the Beginning of This Chapter** – They are some of the best passages to challenge self-limiting beliefs.

6. **Develop a No-Limits Mindset** – Start or increase the habit of challenging concluding statements or thoughts that put limits on you. For instance, if you hear yourself say something like, "Math is difficult for me," then challenge that and ask, "Who told me that?" Note: be careful to not become a "word policeman" correcting every wrong thing people around you say.

Roger Bannister is one person who believed the lid was off. He was the first person to run a mile in less than four minutes (doing so in 1954). The experts had said it was impossible. They said there was a physical lid that prevented human beings from running that fast. Amazingly, within three years of Bannister's feat, ten others did it as well (and now over 1,400 people have run a sub-four-minute mile). When we break through self-imposed limitations, we show others that it's possible to break out of mediocrity and do the same.

As I think about overcoming self-limiting beliefs, I want to give you three more ways to overcome the supposed lids and chains on our lives: mediocre anonymous, worrying with God, and the hearing of faith.

Mediocre Anonymous

I remember when Wendy and I pastored a church in Weaverville, CA, we started a group called Mediocre Anonymous. We did this because we noticed that most twelve-step programs tend to take people from crisis to average, and we wanted to establish a twelve-step program for people addicted to mediocrity to take them from average to great. Here are the tenets and twelve steps:

Believing that those who have believed in Jesus Christ as their personal savior are "born-again" and literally new creatures in Christ, we establish the program of Mediocre Anonymous as a tool to empower and propel people into their destiny and potential.

We are convinced that behaving as "mere men" when we are partakers of a Divine Nature is no longer acceptable. We will determine to pursue a life free from mediocrity or average.

We purpose that this program will not use guilt, anger, or manipulation as a motivational tool. But we will strive to use encouragement, love, and the revealing of talents and gifts within each member of the group.

We will mainly focus on the new behaviors and beliefs that we wish to see manifested in our lives, rather than what is wrong with us.

We commit to anonymity where whatever is shared in a group will stay with the group – whether positive or negative.

12 *Steps For Freedom From Mediocrity*

1. Admit we have not reached our God-given potential.
2. Make a decision to actively pursue the manifestation of His Divine Nature.
3. Allow ourselves to dream of what a life without limitations would look like.
4. Make a fearless inventory of areas or belief systems that put a "lid" or restriction on our lives.
5. Share with God and another person what belief systems or areas we want to war against.

6. Ask God for a revelation of truth concerning those areas that can become weapons of warfare to battle self-limiting beliefs.

7. Make a list of daily declarations based on the truth revealed.

8. Find an action or list of actions that can be implemented to break out of old habit patterns.

9. Sow encouragement in other people's lives to spur them into their destiny.

10. Spend time imagining yourself as successful and unlimited by old 'restraints' or 'lids'.

11. Continue to take personal inventory of wrong identity statements and beliefs.

12. Experiencing new freedom as a result of these steps, we will purpose to not limit others by unforgiveness, negative expectations, or criticisms, but we will purpose to speak encouragement, life, and hope for change in everybody we meet.

Take these twelve steps and meet with your group on a regular basis (60 to 90 minutes is recommended). Here is a good format for you to use in these meetings:

- Determine who is going to lead the meeting. It needs to be someone who is good at facilitating small group discussions and who has a firm understanding of the twelve steps of "Mediocre Anonymous".
- Sit in a circle.
- Open in prayer. Invite God to bless your meetings.
- Have everyone introduce themselves by saying: Hi, my name is _____ and I am an overcover who is overcoming self-limiting beliefs.
- Have someone read the twelve steps out loud.
- Give opportunity for attendees to share testimonies of victories they have had in the past week (especially in the area of beliefs).

- Have assigned reading of one of my books (or another book that focuses on beliefs). I suggest *Victorious Mindsets*, *Igniting Hope in 40 Days*, or *Victorious Emotions* (by Wendy). Have each person share a small excerpt from their reading that stood out to them (one to three sentences is best).
- Discuss what has been shared.
- Take time to speak encouragement to at least one person by telling them the good things you see in them.
- Close in prayer.

The above structure for a small group has great potential to help people reach forward to those things that are ahead for them. For some, it could be a stretch to not primarily focus on what is wrong with them, but the potential benefits are worth the uncomfortable feelings that may be experienced in the process.

Worrying With God

Another tool to increase the likelihood of the hero inside you being released is the habit of worrying with God, instead of worrying with the devil.

Negative worry is imagining your future with God not showing up. Positive worry is seeing your future with God fully showing up. God did not create the imagination to be the devil's playground, so let's use it to be the womb of faith for the "impossible things" God has planned for us.

A University of Cincinnati study discovered that **85% of what we worry about in the negative never happens**, and most people find a successful way to navigate through the 15% that does.

In the 1980s, our church was cursed by a group of witches. They drew a pentagram on the church wall and released a curse over the church. We thought, "If we do not do something to cancel the effects of this curse, bad things are going to happen." We had great faith in the power of the curse. In other words, we were able to worry (or imagine) what life would be like under the influence of that curse.

However, at the same time, when our pastor blessed us at the end of services, we did not have any expectations of good things coming to us. We did not think, "Uh oh, we were just blessed. If we don't cancel the effects of this blessing, we are going to be overtaken with good things happening in our lives." We were unable to even imagine a future where blessing might overtake us or where God would show up supernaturally on our behalf.

We asked ourselves, "Why do we have more faith in the power of a curse than in the power of a blessing?" We realized it was because we were taught about the power of a curse and not the power of a blessing. We also had the tendency of getting our beliefs from our past experiences, rather than from Scripture. This is a habit we were called to overcome.

Wendy and I invented the "Worrying With God" game. If we were blessed by someone, one of us would turn to the other and say, "Oh no, we just got blessed."

Here are some other "worries" we've had with God:

- "What if we get so much energy that we forget to sleep?"
- "What if hospitals forbid us to drive by them because every time we do, all their patients get well and leave?"
- "What if our faces start to shine like Moses' and people demand we wear a veil? Where are we going to be able to buy a full facial veil?"

- "What if our church grows so fast that we need to have ten services a weekend? How will our team be able to handle that?"

Some would say, "This is ridiculous. You need to be more realistic." No, God has not called us to be realistic; He has called us to be supernatural. Even if 85% of what we worry about in the positive never happens, we have much more fun worrying with God than remaining in our negativity.

The Hearing of Faith (The Snoopy Anointing)

Another important attribute of limitless thinkers is they understand the importance of stewarding well what they hear. "Receive not an accusation against an elder except in the mouth of two or three witnesses" (1 Timothy 5:19). This is an incredible verse. It is talking about not lowering your beliefs about people (especially leaders) that you hear unverified, hearsay information about, but there is something deeper in the verse that is encapsulated in the words "receive not". These words tell us we can hear something but not receive it into our spirits (not allow it to negatively affect us). If this is true in the negative, then it is true in the positive by intentionally "receiving" the positive benefits of the life-giving words we hear. This is why Jesus said many times, "He who has ears to hear, let him hear."

We used to have a yellow Labrador named Snoopy. He seemed to sleep all day in our house, but there was one thing that would jolt him out of a deep slumber. It was the moving of his leash on our laundry room shelf. Even if the leash was accidentally and only slightly moved, it didn't matter to Snoopy. When he heard this apparent good news, he bounded into the laundry room and often pulled future walks into his present experience. His incredible hearing caused abundance in his life.

Snoopy illustrated powerful truths about hearing. "Then Jesus said to them, '**Take heed what you hear.** With the same measure you use, it will be measured to you; and **to you who hear, more will be given**. For whoever has, to him more will be given; but whoever does not have, even what he has will be taken away from him'" (Mark 4:24-25). "Therefore **take heed how you hear**. For whoever has, to him more will be given; and whoever does not have, even what he seems to have will be taken from him" (Luke 8:18).

Many of God's people are bound to lack and restriction because they have become dull of hearing. "For indeed the gospel was preached to us as well as to them; but the word which they heard **did not profit them**, not being mixed with faith in those who heard it" (Hebrews 4:2). "Mixing faith" with what we hear is not only how we get into the kingdom, but also how we advance in the kingdom.

The Apostle Paul rebukes the Galatians in Galatians 3:1-5 for becoming more behavior focused than "hearing of faith" focused. "Did you receive the Spirit by the works of the law, or by the hearing of faith? Are you so foolish? Having begun in the Spirit, are you now being made perfect by the flesh?" (Galatians 3:2-3). When we focus more on our behavior than the hearing of faith, we have moved into trying to be made perfect in the flesh. "Therefore He who supplies the Spirit to you and works miracles among you, does He do it by the works of the law, or by the hearing of faith?" (Galatians 3:5). Again, the same way we get into the kingdom is the same way we advance in the kingdom. It is hearing good news and believing it. This is a vital truth for those who want to make high-level, chain-removing, barrier-breaking decisions.

When we prioritize intentionally hearing the good news of the kingdom and mixing faith with it, we set ourselves up for great "profiting" in every area of life. We, like Snoopy, will have our ears tuned for a "jangle in the Spirit" to agree with. To help us walk in this "Snoopy anointing", here are four things we can do to increase the likelihood it will happen:

1. **Recognize it is New Covenant Living** – Galatians 3:1-5 and Romans 10:13-17 confirm this.

2. **Expect to Hear a Life-Prospering Word at Any Moment** – Expectancy is another word for faith. When we expect to hear these "jangles in the Spirit" for our lives, we will increasingly hear them (no matter who the source is).

3. **Be Excited About What You Hear** – Bill Johnson, the senior leader at Bethel Church in Redding, has inspired us to respond with enthusiasm to every testimony we hear. As we train ourselves to get excited about what God has done or is saying, it will help us resist becoming dull of hearing (Hebrews 5:11).

4. **Declare What You Hear** – Jesus declared Himself into victory in Matthew 4:1-11. He spoke Scriptural promises that had been made real to Him. He sets the example for us to declare God's promises over our lives.

These four steps will indeed help you walk in the Snoopy Anointing. I am not sure Snoopy declared things to build his faith and expectancy, but one thing we can say about him is that he was not dull of hearing regarding his leash.

Dullness of hearing is an enemy of great decision-makers. "You have become dull of hearing" (Hebrews 5:11). The Hebrew people allowed themselves to slowly and increasingly become duller to the words which could have radically profited them and those they influenced. Negative strongholds are created when we hear (and mix our faith with) lies more than we hear truth. These strongholds resist hope-filled words because they (the strongholds) are always looking for proof to reinforce already established beliefs.

One of the most important things we can do to be catalytic decision-makers is to resist and overcome dullness of hearing in ourselves. Here are six causes of dullness of hearing and strategies to overcome each one.

1. **Pride** – "And Elisha sent a messenger to him, saying, 'Go and wash in the Jordan seven times, and your flesh shall be restored to you, and you shall be clean.' But Naaman became furious, and went away" (2 Kings 5:10-11). Naaman thought his people and country were superior to the Israelites, thus his judgment and expectations of Elisha's ability were limited by his haughtiness. Remaining humble and teachable is a key to incredible hearing.

2. **Disappointment** – "And their words (about Jesus' resurrection) seemed to them like idle tales, and they did not believe them" (Luke 24:11). Our negative strongholds hate hope. Disappointment creates dullness because we would rather protect ourselves from being disappointed again rather than open up to believing things are and will get better. Even so, we can get healed from this. "He restores my soul" (Psalm 23:3) and the anointing "heals the brokenhearted" (Isaiah 61:1).

3. **Inferiority** – "O my Lord, how can I save Israel? Indeed my clan is the weakest in Manasseh, and I am the least in my father's house" (Judges 6:25). The accuser of the brethren has a whole arsenal of lies to try to keep us feeling unworthy, like a failure, or less than others, and to keep us believing we are the only ones who feel this way. These beliefs try to wear us down and disqualify us from hope. As we feast on our true identity, we can overcome inferiority and actually hear the potential for our lives.

4. **Traditions of Men Doctrines** – "Making the word of God of no effect through your tradition which you have handed down." (Mark 7:13). The Pharisees in the gospels and Book of Acts could not hear what God was really saying because it did not fit into their man-made doctrinal beliefs. When we overemphasize the sovereignty of God and the works of the law, we create a doctrinal dullness that makes us passive, fatalistic, and fixated on a lifestyle of sin-avoidance over greatness-building.

5. **Familiarity** – "'Is this not the carpenter, the Son of Mary, and brother of James, Joses, Judas, and Simon? And are not His sisters here with us?' So they were offended at Him" (Mark 6:3). If we are not careful, we can allow our familiarity with a person, a ministry, a truth, the prophetic, or a type of testimony to cause us to lose the wonder of these things, contributing to dullness of hearing. Honor is the antidote to this. "'Honor your father and mother,' which is the first commandment with promise: 'that it may be well with you and you may live long on the earth'" (Ephesians 6:2-3).

6. **Weariness** – "And let us not grow weary while doing good, for in due season we shall reap if we do not lose heart" (Galatians 6:9). When we are tired, it is more challenging for us to hear. Sometimes my dog, Buddy, won't hear me come into the house because of how tired he is, even though he has positioned himself to always hear the good news of his master's return. After a good rest, he is able to hear at a higher level. Some of us just need a good nap or extra rest to tune up our spiritual hearing.

As we recognize these dullness creators, we can overcome them and mix our faith with what we hear in order to experience increase. We will know we are entering into incredible hearing when we hear with hope—the belief the future will be better than the present and we have the power to help make it so.

Conclusion

We cannot be great decision-makers if we are living in survivalism, self-protection, passivity, fatalism, believing we are destined to be average, or if we believe what we are experiencing is what God wants us to experience. Yes, we are thankful for where we are at and what we have now, but we will not settle and believe this is all there is. "Father, if You wanted us to think small and with limitations, you sure did a bad job in telling us so." Because of this, we will press into "the more", and this will radically and positively impact the type of decisions we will make in the days and years ahead.

CHAPTER 8

Breaking Out of the Pack

"My servant Caleb . . . has a different spirit in him" (Numbers 14:24).

I enjoy watching track and field events. Here is a frequent scenario I have observed. There will be a pack of runners seemingly clumped together going at the same pace. Then there will be one runner with a burst of speed who separates himself from the others, takes the lead, and wins. This runner broke out of the pack.

Caleb "broke out of the pack" of the people he was connected to. He had a "different spirit". He and Joshua were the only ones from his generation to actually enter the Promised Land.

This is a "break out the pack book". The concept of using cheerfulness as an indicator that we have attached faith to what we have decided to do is life-changing. And as we pursue being fully convinced concerning our identity and choices, we will be energized to be a Caleb (one who has a "different spirit") to our generation.

In this chapter, we will target three areas that will take us higher in our decision-making (and which will help those around us make powerful choices as well):

- Attaching faith to our relationships with people
- Getting buy-in from others in our decisions
- Committing to a lifestyle of encouragement

Attaching Faith to Our Relationships With People ("I Choose You Again")

One of the most important areas where we make decisions is regarding the people who will be in our lives. Now, certainly, there are many people in our lives that we do not have a choice about - our family, who our parents are/were, who our siblings are, our extended family, those that live in our neighborhood, those that we go to school with, those in the same church as us, etc. But we also get to choose, even in those relationships, how much we invest in those people, and what level of priority they are to us.

Who are the people that are closest to you? Jesus had the one (John). He had the three (Peter James, and John). He had the twelve (his disciples). He had the 72 (see Luke 10). He had wider groups of relationships (the 500 who saw him after his resurrection and the 5,000 who were supernaturally fed). Who are the people in your inner circle and outer circle? Some of our most important decisions concern who we prioritize in our relationships.

We cannot give ourselves equally to everybody. We need boundaries in relationships. We are not called to give to every need that is presented to us because we have priority commitments we are to invest our time, energy, and resources into. For me, my marriage is the number one earthly relationship I have, followed by my children and grandchildren. And even though the nature of family relationships changes, I still choose them again and again as the most important.

An important concept in relationships for me is encapsulated in these words, "I choose you again." In marriage vows, we are basically saying, "I will choose you over and over no matter what happens." It is an ongoing recommitment that is also to be implemented in other relationships.

Before I continue in this thought, let's talk about a big reason we withdraw our hearts from people, and thus no longer attach faith to our relationship with them. The nature of most relationships is this: 1) excitement, 2) disappointment, and 3) then either reconnection or disconnection. This is true in marriage, friendships, jobs, and with leaders, employees, churches, roommates, volunteers for our organizations, etc. When disappointment comes, it presents some of the most crucial moments to help us build catalytic decision-making muscles. If we have the tendency to doubt or feel victimized by a relationship, we will not break out of the pack to become exceptional in what we do or decide. It is in these times of disappointment that we get to say to ourselves, "I choose them again! I attach faith to this relationship." Yes, there will be times when we will need to clarify our options about a certain relationship (and potentially change the nature of the relationship), but we cannot allow our disappointments to linger and cause us to live in doubt, passivity, or reluctance concerning them.

"I choose you again!" Who do you need to choose again today? What relationships have you allowed disappointment to cause you to move into passivity, victimhood, doubt, or disconnection? Are there relationships you are prioritizing that shouldn't be prioritized? Who are the people you need to choose at a higher level? Who do you need to choose again (or choose for the first time) and then attach faith to that relationship through making powerful declarations like this:

- I choose _____ again.
- God has a high purpose for this relationship.

- I will not withdraw my heart from this person but will bring myself fully into the relationship.
- I am committed to serving the dreams of this person.
- I will be empowered by God to handle challenges in this relationship well.
- I am not codependent on this person. They are not responsible for my joy and happiness. I will thrive no matter what they do.
- I will continually confess my hope without wavering when it comes to this relationship.
- I will regularly consider how to stir up encouragement regarding this person.
- I have increasing cheerfulness when I am around _____.

Including Others and Getting Buy-in for Your Decisions

Leaders, parents, and influencers who decide things alone and then announce their decisions to those they are leading are much less likely to have healthy relationships than those who have a proactive plan to include others in their decision-making. Wise leaders understand how to get buy-in from key people who are going to be influenced by their decisions.

We are not called to make decisions in isolation. "In the multitude of counselors there is safety" (Proverbs 11:14). We need other people (mentors, leaders, spouses, and others) to be a part of the important decisions we make. This creates "safety" for us because as we listen to different viewpoints, the likelihood of making poor decisions will decrease. This is especially true when our emotions or desires are clouding good judgment.

Now, as we consider getting buy-in from people, I want to say this again: as a leader, it is very unwise to just decide something and then announce the decision. I have worked in the church and with various teams for many years, and I have not always done this right. I have felt the pain when I haven't consulted the right people, or when I haven't gone through a good process to increase the likelihood of people being able to agree, accept, and support my decision.

I remember listening to John Maxwell describing his leadership team (his board) in his first pastorate in Ohio. He said early on in his leadership there, he would go into a meeting with an idea or a direction, and he soon discovered that there was one board member who was the strongest voice the others listened to. Maxwell realized if that board member was not in favor of what he was doing, then the likelihood of his direction, vision, or thought being implemented was slim. So he planned to meet with that board member to bounce off his ideas to get a feel for what might be concerns, resistance, or fears that he was not aware of that he would need to proactively address. And so he developed the habit of coming to the rest of the board members with his work already done. I believe this is such a great principle for business leaders, church leaders, managers, parents, etc. to have already "tested the waters" on certain things, especially major directions and changes before presenting a final decision. In my opinion, most pushback against new ideas and new directions can be avoided through proactive communication and pursuing buy-in prior to the meeting where these new changes are officially presented. Certainly, there are some situations where this is not possible, and the leader has to take a stand for specific directions, but that type of circumstance is going to be infrequent compared to what I am describing now.

Let's take this discussion on buy-in further. When we are planning a change in direction that will impact others, here's a good plan of how to move it forward. **First of all, float the idea to individuals or groups.** Plant the seed of a potential change in people's thinking by saying something like, "I'm thinking about hiring somebody for this position. I don't know yet if that is the direction we will take, but I'm just thinking about it." Or, "I've thought about us working four days a week instead of five days. I don't know if that's where we need to go, but I've just had that thought, and I've heard of other businesses where that's been done successfully." You throw the idea out there and see what happens. Here is another one, "Family, I was thinking about doing an extended visit at grandma's this summer. I don't know if it's going to happen but I am wondering if we should." (You may need to hold off floating this idea to very young children who love grandma - ha.) So that's the seed planting or floating ideas stage.

Next, is the "testing the waters" stage where we actually talk with key influencers regarding the decision and those who are going to be influenced by the decision. For instance, if I'm the pastor of a church and I want to paint the nursery, I will need to include, at the very least, the nursery director in this. It would be foolish to not do so. The "testing the waters" conversation would go something like this, "I am still thinking of this. What do you think about it?"

The third step in these buy-in conversations is having deeper personal and small group conversations about the matter. Who is included in these communications depends on how big the decision is. If it is a big decision, you will want to talk to the organization's core leaders. These are the conversations where you indicate what you are believing regarding the proposed changes. Again, you will need to talk to key influencers who may not be directly involved or affected by the decision, but who are connected at a relational level to people that may be.

Finally, the direction is discussed and finalized at an official meeting of the organization or family with wording like, "WE have decided to do this."

These steps will save leaders, parents, and bosses from many heartaches. Pursuing buy-in is a key component of decision-making. It includes the right people in the process of making decisions.

By the way, the process of pursuing buy-in will often reveal whether the direction you wanted to go was a bad direction or a good one based on the feedback on things that you hadn't considered. So, it's part of the process of creating and maintaining safety in a multitude of counselors.

One final thought on pursuing buy-in from others. As we seek to do this, it will become more clear if the people around you buy-in to you as a person. This is the ultimate buy-in that will make all other buy-ins easier.

Do people trust you? If not, then addressing and correcting reasons people might question you is more important than the decision to be made. "What can I do to help you trust me more?" This pursuit of building trust will cause the ultimate buy-in (to you as a person). It will create deeper heart connections with people which will make unity in decisions much more likely.

Encouraging and Building People

One of the ways to break out of the pack is to prioritize encouraging and building people up. The first thing I have in my bio is that Steve Backlund is an encourager. I would rather be known as an encourager than an intergalactic apostle. Barnabas, whose name means "son of encouragement", is one of my biblical heroes. Without him, there probably would not have been an Apostle Paul. His words strengthened the decision-making of Saul (who would become Paul), and it caused the other Apostles to decide to accept him. "And when Saul had come to Jerusalem, he tried to join the disciples; but they were all afraid of him, and did not believe that he was a disciple. **But Barnabas** took him and brought him to the apostles. And he declared to them how he had seen the Lord on the road, and that He had spoken to him, and how he had preached boldly at Damascus in the name of Jesus. So he was with them at Jerusalem, coming in and going out" (Acts 9:26-28).

Those who commit to the ministry of encouragement will not only help the decision-making of others but will also go higher in their own decision-making. Jesus said the greatest of you would be the servant of all. One of the main ways we can serve other people is to encourage them in their giftings, their endurance, their beliefs, and in other ways.

Hebrews 10:23-25 are some of my favorite verses on the subject of encouragement. "Let us hold fast the confession of our hope without wavering, for he who promised is faithful. And let us consider how to stir up one another to love and good works, not neglecting to meet together, as is the habit of some, but encouraging one another, and all the more as you see the Day drawing near" (ESV). This reveals three levels of encouragement: 1) Encouraging Ourselves, 2) Encouraging Others, and 3) Increasing Encouragement.

1. Encourage Ourselves

"Let us hold fast the confession of our hope without wavering, for He who promised is faithful" (Hebrews 10:23).

This verse implores us to a continual "confession" of hope, and it tells us why: "for He who promised is faithful." The more I believe He is faithful, the more hope I will confess. I am not into positive thinking, but I am a proponent of biblical optimism. Hope is the belief that the future will be better than the present, and I/we have the power to help make it so.

The most important person we need to encourage is ourselves. "But David strengthened (encouraged) himself in the Lord his God" (1 Samuel

30:6). One of the main ways we encourage ourselves is to declare God's promises concerning our abilities, our identity, and our circumstances.

2. Encourage Others

"And let us consider how to stir up one another to love and good works" (Hebrews 10:24).

One of the greatest decisions we can make is to regularly "consider" others. I believe a great question in this biblical considering of others is, "What do I like about them?" As we ponder this question, we will develop more of a father-heart for people, which will enable our influence and leadership to be healthy.

Let me expand on this. In Luke 15 there are three main characters. First, there is the prodigal son; second, the father; and third, the elder brother. The prodigal son is mentioned most in the story, but I want to look at the attitudes of both the father and elder brother to give us insights into this "considering" others. How they saw the prodigal son reflected a "default" mindset about people and life.

The default of the "elder brother mindset" is to first see what is wrong with a person or place. The default of a "father mindset" is to first see what is right with a person or place. God will take us all on a journey of moving us from having an elder brother attitude to having a father's heart. As we grow in this, we will be entrusted more and more to lead His people.

We cannot break out of the pack in decision-making if we have elder brother attitudes of pride, entitlement, jealousy, competition, separation, and performance. We will suppress our own potential and become part of the problem in people's lives, rather than a solution.

"Not neglecting to meet together, as is the habit of some, but encouraging one another."

One of the main reasons we gather together in the body of Christ is to encourage one another. As we consider one another from a father's perspective and then share what we see, we will put courage into lives. We are to make it our goal to find people to encourage in every gathering we attend. Indeed, there is no such thing as the strong silent type of Christian.

I used to not want to encourage people around me who had faults because I thought if I encouraged them, they would stop working on their faults. This attitude worked against me and the relationships I had. I know from my own experience that we can more easily receive correction from someone who sees the good in us, than one who just sees our faults.

3. Increase Encouragement

"And (encourage) all the more as you see the Day drawing near" (Hebrews 10:25).

Whatever you believe "the Day" means theologically, it is getting nearer. And, as we see it getting nearer, we are to continually increase our encouragement (our speaking hope) in quantity and quality.

Quality encouragement is called prophetic ministry. It is the spiritual gift to be desired most (1 Corinthians 14:1). The gift of prophecy in the New Testament is encouraging ("but he who prophesies speaks edification and exhortation and comfort to men" - 1 Corinthians 14:3). It is not the same as the five-fold office of the prophet who brings correction, and specific direction (Ephesians 4:11-16), but the gift of prophecy (that we can all function in) speaks life and encouragement to people.

"Steve, how can I learn to prophesy?" Here's my answer: become the most encouraging person you know and ask the Holy Spirit to take over your encouragement. When you do, God will take you on a journey of being an incredible difference maker in people's lives which will cause others to have breakthroughs and make decisions they never thought possible.

Here is more proof about the power of encouragement from Isaiah 35:4-6: "Say to those who are fearful-hearted, 'Be strong, do not fear! Behold, your God will . . . come . . . and save you.' Then the eyes of the blind shall be opened, and the ears of the deaf shall be unstopped. Then the lame shall leap like a deer." As we speak encouraging words to the fearful-hearted (including ourselves), we will help create supernatural breakthroughs all around us.

We can break out of the pack by being a radical encourager to:

- Ourselves - Again, the most important person I need to prophesy to and encourage is me. I have written a number of books on making declarations that will help you understand the why and how of this.
- Our family and the people who are closest to us - Those who do not let familiarity and disappointment dampen their encouragement are rare. They have truly become thermostats and not thermometers.
- Leaders over us - We live in a time where honor and respect for leaders is decreasing. Let's resist this tendency and become a strength to the leaders around us.
- Those we are assigned to - It is important in life to identify the people we feel called to and find ways to be an encouraging voice to them.
- Divine appointment situations - Look for unusual coincidences and people highlighted to speak to.

Three Final Questions

1. When Is It Okay to Change Our Minds About a Decision We Have Made?

There will be times when we'll change our minds concerning something we previously decided to do. Abraham changed his mind when he was planning to sacrifice Isaac, but then didn't (Genesis 22). In Acts 10, Peter changed his mind about fellowshipping with Gentiles and eating certain foods. Joseph changed his mind when he was planning to leave his relationship with Mary and instead, decided to stay with her (Matthew 1:20). Even God changed his mind because of Moses' intercession (Number 14).

I speak a lot about attaching faith and staying in faith concerning decisions and what we believe we have heard the Lord say. It is vital we learn to remain fully convinced even in the face of contrary circumstances and contrary emotions. This is an important part of having strong beliefs and increased load-bearing capacity. If we easily change our minds because of emotions, pressure from people, or impulsive tendencies, we will be greatly hindered in reaching our potential. It is vital to remember that how we make decisions is almost always more important than the decisions we make.

So when do we change our minds? Certainly, with smaller things in life, it doesn't really matter if we make a change in what we do (e.g. whether we change the brand of vegetable we buy or not). But in the bigger things of life (in relationship choices, callings, financial issues, etc.), we acknowledge we can reverse a previous decision or commitment, but we must do so carefully and we must follow a healthy process in doing so.

If we begin to feel a stirring internally that we might need to change our minds about something, we need to go back to our decision-making process and clarify our options again. We will have to look at the originally decided upon option, and then the other options that would be classified under the changing of the mind. After this, we will need to go through the same steps (detailed earlier in the book) again then conclude what we are to do and attach faith to it. When we go through this process, we will protect ourselves from making emotion-based decisions, pressure-based decisions, or "fear of missing out" based decisions.

2. What Important Truths Are to be Remembered From This Book?

Here are some of the most important points:

1. A bad decision made in faith has a greater likelihood of success than a good decision made in doubt.
2. Cheerfulness is a main evidence we have attached faith to what we are doing.
3. Most people's tiredness is spiritual (from doubt, doing things out of duty, etc.), not physical.
4. We don't wait until we are doing something great to attach great faith, but we attach great faith to what we are doing now and it becomes great.
5. A double-minded man is unstable in all his ways.
6. If I believe I am significant and what I am doing is significant, then I am significant and so is what I am doing.
7. The anxiety concerning not knowing what to do is a bigger concern than the decision itself.
8. James 1:5 is the "tracking number" that tells us wisdom is coming and that we will always know what to do.
9. "Let each be fully convinced in his own mind" (Romans 14:5).

10. "Abraham was strengthened in faith, giving glory to God, and being fully convinced that what He had promised He was also able to perform" (Romans 4:20-21).
11. Those who succeed most also seem to fail most.
12. How we make decisions is more important than the decisions we make.
13. The greatest beliefs we need to have will sound ridiculous when we first hear them.

3. What Can I Do to Keep Growing in Becoming Fully Convinced?

1. Create a group to read through this book together.
2. Enroll in Igniting Hope's 8-week online course, "Fully Convinced", on www.ignitinghopeacademy.com. The videos and podcasts will take your readings to another level.
3. Re-read a chapter a week for the next eight weeks.

APPENDIX - DECISION CHART

	Option A	Option B
Options		
Pros		
Cons		
Scriptures		
Prophetic Words		
Dreams		
God Stories		
Counsel		
Peace Level		
Conclusion		

APPENDIX - BELIEFS TO DECLARE TO INCREASE YOUR STRENGTH AND INFLUENCE

1. **The Adaptability Belief** – I will thrive no matter what happens. (Philippians 4:11-13)

2. **The Hope Belief** – I believe the future will be better than the present and I have the power to help make it so. (Romans 15:13; Jeremiah 29:4-11)

3. **The Faith Belief** – I am thankful that God's promises and my past prayers are working in my life, my family's lives, my circumstances, and my nation. (Hebrews 11:1)

4. **The Forgiveness Belief** – My intentional forgiveness creates well-being for others and for me. (Luke 23:34; Acts 7:60-8:1)

5. **The Long-Term Thinking Belief** – My beliefs and choices are leaving a positive legacy for generations to come. (Hebrews 11:20)

6. **The Joy and Laughter Belief** – I have strength and longevity because I consistently activate joy and laughter in my life. (Nehemiah 8:10; Proverbs 17:22)

7. **The Solutions Belief** – In every situation I face, I have many options, solutions, and divine ideas. There is always a solution. (1 Corinthians 10:13; James 1:5)

8. **The Beliefs About Others** – I see people according to their potential, not according to their past. (2 Corinthians 5:16; Judges 6:12)

9. **The Soul Prosperity Belief** – My response to something is almost always more important than the something. (3 John 2)

10. **The "Bottom-Lining" Belief** – Even if the worst happens, I will be okay. (Daniel 3:16-18)

11. **The Training Focus Belief** – My current challenges and frustrations are my training ground for the greater influence I will have in the future. (James 1:2-5; Romans 5:3-4; Psalm 119:71)

12. **The Peace Belief**– Peace is one of my strongest weapons in prayer. (Philippians 4:6-7; Romans 16:20)

13. **The Follow Through and Integrity Belief** – I make commitments with forethought, and I follow through on what I say I will do. (Matthew 5:37; Psalm 15:4b)

14. **The Imagination Belief**– I use my imagination to activate my faith. (2 Corinthians 4:18)

15. **The Identity Belief** – I am not who my past says I am; I am who God says I am.(2 Corinthians 5:17; Hebrews 10:14)

16. **The Staying Relational Belief** – I will not withdraw my heart from people who disappoint me or that I hear negative information about. (1 Corinthians 13:4-7; 1 Timothy 5:19) (This does not mean that at times we won't have boundaries in relationships.)

17. **The Forward Movement Belief** – My forward movement in life causes Red Seas to part. (Exodus 14:15-21; Philippians 3:13)

18. **The Courage Belief** – I am brave and run at my Goliaths. (1 Samuel 17:48)

19. **The Authenticity Belief** – My authenticity connects my heart to people and gives them hope. (Philippians 3:12; 1 Peter 5:5-6)

20. **The Unique Purpose Belief** – I understand my assignment and giftings, and I know what God's called me to do and not to do. (Romans 12:4-8; 1 Peter 4:10-11)

21. **The Decision-Making Belief** – I am a great decision maker and attach faith to every decision I make. (Romans 14:5; James 1:5)

22. **The Being Loved by God Belief** – I am unconditionally loved by God and worthy to receive love and blessings today. (1 John 4:19; Luke 15:20)

23. **The Valuing Process Belief** – I don't wait for perfection to celebrate myself and be joyful. (Philippians 3:12-14)

24. **The Encouraging Others Belief** – I radically encourage others daily. (Hebrews 10:24-25; Hebrews 3:13)

25. **The Spiritual Laws Belief** – I honor God's spiritual laws therefore I increase in favor, finance, health, and happiness. (Joshua 1:8; Psalm 1:2-3)

APPENDIX ADDITIONAL RESOURCES

VICTORIOUS MINDSETS

What we believe is ultimately more important than what we do. The course of our lives is set by our deepest core beliefs. Our mindsets are either a stronghold for God's purposes or a playhouse for the enemy. In this book, ffty biblical attitudes are revealed that are foundational for those who desire to walk in freedom and power.

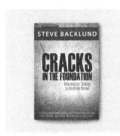

CRACKS IN THE FOUNDATION

Going to a higher level in establishing key beliefs will affect ones intimacy with God and fruitfulness for the days ahead. This book challenges many basic assumptions of familiar Bible verses and common Christian phrases that block numerous benefits of our salvation. The truths shared in this book will help fill and repair "cracks" in our thinking which rob us of our God-given potential. Revised edition includes upgraded content, study questions, and declarations.

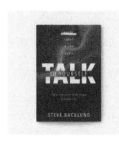

YOU'RE CRAZY IF YOU DON'T TALK TO YOURSELF

Jesus did not just think His way out of the wilderness and neither can we. He spoke truth to invisible beings and mindsets that sought to restrict and defeat Him. This book reveals that life and death are truly in the power of the tongue, and emphasize the necessity of speaking truth to our souls. Our words really do set the course of our lives and the lives of others (Proverbs 18:21, James 3:2-5).

LET'S JUST LAUGH AT THAT

Our hope level is an indicator of whether we are believing truth or lies. Truth creates hope and freedom, but believing lies brings hopelessness and restriction. We can have great theology but still be powerless because of deception about the key issues of life. Many of these self-defeating mindsets exist in our subconscious and have never been identified. This book exposes numerous falsehoods and reveals truth that makes us free. Get ready for a joy-infused adventure into hope-filled living.

IGNITING FAITH IN 40 DAYS

There must be special seasons in our lives when we break out of routine and do something that will ignite our faith about God and our identity in Christ. This book will lead you through the life-changing experience of a 40-day negativity fast. This fast teaches the power of declaring truth and other transforming daily customs that will strengthen your foundation of faith and radically increase your personal hope.

LIVING FROM THE UNSEEN

This book will help you identify beliefs that block the reception of God's blessings and hinder our ability to live out our destiny. This book reveals that 1) Believing differently, not trying harder, is the key to change; 2) You cannot do what you don't believe you are; 3) You can only receive what you think you are worth; 4) Rather than learning how to die — it is time to learn how to live.

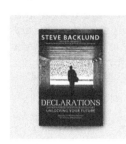

DECLARATIONS: UNLOCKING YOUR FUTURE

You may be wondering, "What are declarations and why are people making them?" or maybe, "Aren't declarations simply a repackaged 'name it and claim' heresy?" Declarations answers these questions by sharing 30 biblical reasons for declaring truth over every area of life. Steve Backlund and his team also answer common objections and concerns to the teaching about declarations. The revelation this book carries will help you to set the direction your life will go.

DECLARE IT: INCLUDES DECLARATIONS FOR 96 DIFFERENT LIFE SITUATIONS

If we are going to experience something higher, we need to believe something higher. If we are going to believe something higher, we need to hear something higher than what we are feeling and experiencing. Declarations are faith statements about what is true but is not fully yet in our experience. One of the greatest ways to activate our faith and renew our minds is to declare truth. This book provides powerful, biblically-based truths to declare for almost every conceivable situation we will face in life.

IGNITING HOPE IN 40 DAYS

This book will truly ignite your hope. We believe you will become convinced that hope is the belief that the future will be better than the present, and you have the power to help make it so Our hope level determines our influence level. Our hopelessness about a problem is a bigger problem than the problem. And so much more. Join Steve on a 40-Day journey to spark your faith and hope into higher levels than ever before!

HELP! I'M A PASTOR

This book is practical, revelatory, and humorous, with 50 common scenarios that could cause a pastor to say, "They didn't prepare me for this in Bible school!" HELP! I'm A Pastor replaces exasperation with expectation using 80 life and leadership core values to tackle situations including: My People Are Always Late For Meetings, I Am Tempted To Have An Affair, How Transparent Is Too Transparent?, and Pastor, She Is A Jezebel.

LET'S JUST LAUGH AT THAT FOR KIDS!
We all want the best for the young people in our lives. This book will help you set children up for success by teaching them to replace lies with truth and to take a combative stance against beliefs that try to hold them back. This book is an interactive journey in taking every thought captive with the kids you love. Through these fun, laughter–filled pages, we expose twenty common lies kids often believe, and this book helps train them to use "laughter weapons" to disarm the lies. We then use Scripture, declarations, and practical wisdom to reinforce the truth.

THE CULTURE OF EMPOWERMENT
Have you ever been championed by someone? Their belief in you became a rock to stand on against the waves of insecurity, doubt, and fear in your mind.. This book reveals a solid biblical foundation for living a lifestyle of empowerment. Through empowering people, Jesus set an example for us and revealed the Father's heart in doing so. The Culture of Empowerment gives insight and practical tools for championing people as well as developing empowering beliefs about yourself and others.

VICTORIOUS EMOTIONS
Are you tired of trying hard to be happy and victorious? Are you tired of working hard at enjoying life? Then this book is for you. Victorious Emotions will help create happiness as your default emotion. Even if we have unhappy circumstances, we can build a system of beliefs that, as effortless as the tides, will always bring us back to joy. This book gives powerful, practical strategies to live out Romans 12:2, which says to be transformed by the renewing of the mind. It is time to be overtaken by emotions that lead us into victory!

THE CULTURE OF EMPOWERMENT: BUSINESS AND ORGANIZATION EDITION

Whether you're a business owner, church small group leader, family leader, or in some area of influence, the absolute fastest way to make your visions for the future become your reality is to become an empowering leader. More than staff education, more than going to conferences, more than getting another degree on your wall, becoming an empowering leader who inspires and equips others is the best way to make your dreams reality.

Made in the USA
Las Vegas, NV
17 April 2023

70709179R00090